the adult years

HUMAN BEHAVIOR

the adult years

BY WILBUR BRADBURY

AND THE EDITORS OF TIME-LIFE BOOKS

TIME-LIFE BOOKS, NEW YORK

The Author: Wilbur Bradbury is a freelance
science writer and the author of a novel,
Your Golden Jugular. He has been a sports writer
for *The New York Times* and served as a science
editor of LIFE. With his wife and two children,
he lives in New York City.

General Consultants for Human Behavior:
Robert M. Krauss is Professor of Psychology at
Columbia University. He has taught at Princeton
and Harvard and was Chairman of the Psychology
Department at Rutgers. He is the co-author of
Theories in Social Psychology, edits the *Journal of
Experimental Social Psychology* and contributes
articles to many journals on aspects of human
behavior and social interaction.

Peter I. Rose, a specialist on racial and ethnic
relations, is Sophia Smith Professor of Sociology
and Anthropology at Smith College and is on the
graduate faculty of the University of Massachusetts.
His books include *They and We, The Subject Is
Race* and *Americans from Africa.* Professor Rose
has also taught at Goucher, Wesleyan, Colorado,
Clark, Yale, Amherst, the University of Leicester in
England, Kyoto University in Japan and Flinders
University in Australia.

James W. Fernandez is Professor of Anthropology
at Princeton University. His research in culture
change has taken him to East, West and South
Africa and the Iberian peninsula. Articles on his
field studies have been widely published in
European and American anthropology journals. He
has been president of the Northeastern
Anthropological Association and a consultant to the
Foreign Service Institute.

Special Consultants for The Adult Years:
Daniel J. Levinson, a social psychologist whose
academic interests include sociology and
anthropology, taught at Harvard for 16 years and is
now a professor of psychology at Yale University.
Besides publishing articles in professional journals,
he is co-author of several books, including *The
Authoritarian Personality, Patienthood in the
Mental Hospital* and *The Executive Role
Constellation.*

M. Powell Lawton is a psychologist and the director
of behavioral research at the Philadelphia Geriatric
Center in Pennsylvania. He has published several
books and articles on the aged, including *The
Psychology of Adult Development* and *Aging,* of
which he is co-editor, and *Planning and Managing
Housing for the Elderly.*

TIME-LIFE BOOKS

FOUNDER: Henry R. Luce 1898-1967

Editor-in-Chief: Hedley Donovan
Chairman of the Board: Andrew Heiskell
President: James R. Shepley

Vice Chairman: Roy E. Larsen

MANAGING EDITOR: Jerry Korn
Assistant Managing Editors: Ezra Bowen,
David Maness, Martin Mann, A. B. C. Whipple
Planning Director: Oliver E. Allen
Art Director: Sheldon Cotler
Chief of Research: Beatrice T. Dobie
Director of Photography: Melvin L. Scott
Senior Text Editors: Diana Hirsh, William Frankel
Assistant Planning Director: Carlotta Kerwin
Assistant Art Director: Arnold C. Holeywell
Assistant Chief of Research: Myra Mangan

PUBLISHER: Joan D. Manley
General Manager: John D. McSweeney
Business Manager: John Steven Maxwell
Sales Director: Carl G. Jaeger
Promotion Director: Paul R. Stewart
Public Relations Director: Nicholas Benton

HUMAN BEHAVIOR
Editorial Staff for *The Adult Years:*
EDITOR: William K. Goolrick
Assistant Editor: Carole Kismaric
Text Editor: Virginia Adams
Picture Editor: Adrian Allen
Designer: John Martinez
Assistant Designer: Marion Flynn
Staff Writers: Richard Cravens, Simone Gossner,
Suzanne Seixas
Chief Researcher: Barbara Ensrud
Researchers: Oscar C. K. Chiang, Barbara Fleming,
Dunstan Harris, Gail Nussbaum, Fred Ritchin,
Constance R. Roosevelt

Editorial Production
Production Editor: Douglas B. Graham
Assistant Production Editors:
Gennaro C. Esposito, Feliciano Madrid
Quality Director: Robert L. Young
Assistant Quality Director: James J. Cox
Associate: Serafino J. Cambareri
Copy Staff: Eleanore W. Karsten (chief),
Susan B. Galloway, Georgia Ingersoll,
Florence Keith, Pearl Sverdlin
Picture Department: Dolores A. Littles,
Jessy Faubert, Joan Lynch
Traffic: Carmen McLellan

Valuable assistance was given by the following departments and individuals of Time Inc.: Editorial
Production, Norman Airey; Library, Benjamin Lightman; Picture Collection, Doris O'Neil;
Photographic Laboratory, George Karas; TIME-LIFE News Service, Murray J. Gart;
Correspondents Ann Natanson and Deborah Sgardello (Rome), Margot Hapgood and
Dorothy Bacon (London), Maria Vincenza Aloisi and Josephine du Brusle (Paris),
Elisabeth Kraemer and Franz Spelman (Bonn), S. Chang and Frank Iwama (Tokyo),
Sue Masterman (The Hague), Bing Wong (Hong Kong).

Contents

Growth: Lifelong Cycle

1

"The process is not like climbing up a hill and down the other side, but more akin to a Himalayan expedition during which camps must be made at varying altitudes, guides found, the terrain explored, skills acquired, rests taken before moving up to the next level. . . . The descent is also made in stages." This is psychoanalyst Theodore Lidz speaking, and he is talking about the course of the life cycle—describing what it is like to grow from infancy into adulthood and then to descend gradually toward death.

Scientific study of the life cycle is a new phenomenon, and Lidz is one of the first experts in human behavior to write a detailed account of the human progress through life. The chief reason most earlier scientists paid little attention to life as a whole is simple. Development during childhood is so rapid, so readily distinguishable into stages and so clearly significant for later life that it occupied most attention. It mesmerized some scientists, who came to believe that human development ends with childhood. The progression from birth to death seemed, as Lidz intimated, rather like hiking up a hill to reach adulthood and then taking an uneventful walk across a plateau that remained level—and barren of scientifically interesting scenery—until the path dipped downward toward the close of life's journey.

Now scientists know life is more dynamic than that. They recognize that although human development is most dramatic in early life, it does not end at the age of four or six or eight. Within any segment of the population—such as the Pennsylvania farm family at left—development occurs in every age group. Sociologist John Clausen even suggests that one human may, in effect, be many different people in his lifetime. These changes after childhood occur at discernible stages: adolescence, young adulthood, the middle years and old age. The stages seem the same for everyone in a culture, and what happens in each stage generally happens to everyone at about that time. For example, just as most babies walk at the age of one and talk at two, most Westerners grapple with the choice of a mate in their twenties, agonize over the meaning of their lives in their forties, and suffer crises of self-confidence in their fifties. Yet as striking as the similarity of such behavior within a culture is the difference between cultures. The lines dividing the stages of life, so sharply drawn among some peoples, may be blurred or almost missing among others, and the experiences within each stage totally unalike.

Scientific interest in the life cycle has grown out of several factors. Perhaps one of the most significant is the dramatic lengthening of the human life span that has occurred since 1900. Consider just two examples. In Japan the average life expectancy in 1900 for males was 43.97 years, for females 44.85; by 1973 it had risen to 70.70 and 76.02 respectively. In the United States the life-expectancy figure for both sexes was 49 in the earlier year, compared with 71 in the later one. By 1975 men and women over the age of 60 made up 15 per cent of the entire population in the United States; in England, France, Germany, Italy and Japan, the respective figures were 19.3 per cent, 18 per cent, 20.6 per cent, 17.2 per cent and 11.7 per cent.

Since simply being old poses many problems—for the elderly, for their relatives and for society itself—the very existence of a large number of oldsters has inevitably caused the experts to pay attention to them and has led to the development of the new science of gerontology. But a growing aged population is not in itself enough to create interest in the whole life span.

However, a growing population of the aged is only the most obvious aspect of a phenomenon that has only recently begun to be appreciated. Age distribution—the proportions of a total population that lie within various age groups—varies markedly from nation to nation, and even more important, changes markedly over time within a nation. West Germany, for example, has the world's highest proportion of elderly people, Pakistan the highest proportion of young people, and Japan an unusually high proportion of middle-aged persons *(page 11)*.

Even more remarkable are the strange and dramatic ways these population proportions may shift. In the United States during the decade of the 1970s, the population as a whole is expected to increase by 11.2 per cent. The proportion of people between the ages of 0 and 20 will go up by only 0.3 per cent, but the 20 to 40 age group will increase by 33.7 per cent. The 40 to 60 segment will not change, but the proportion of people over 60 will go up by 15.9 per cent. The effects on society—in schools to be built or closed, the number and kinds of jobs needed, the medical and social services to be provided—are profound. With such major issues being raised, it is not surprising scientists began to look beyond the earliest years for the principles governing human behavior. Bernice Neugarten, a pioneer in the new life-cycle field, used a vivid figure of speech to make the point: "Seated under the same circus tent, some of us who are child psychologists remain seated too close to the entrance and are missing much of the action that is going on in the main ring. Others of us who are gerontologists remain seated too close to the exit. Both groups are missing a view of the whole show."

Contemporary scientists who determined to get a better perspective on "the whole show" were actually picking up a concern of ancient prophets, philosophers and writers, many of whom set down their views about the life cycle. "Birth, death, growth and decline are, in fact, too conspicuous to have been overlooked by any culture," sociologist Karl Groffman observes. But the old descriptions of life phases often differ in important ways from those formulated by 20th Century researchers. Usually they portray each period as linked to one specific age. Many modern theories, by contrast, emphasize that although the stages of life follow one another in a regular order that does not vary from person to person, these stages occur at different ages in different people; adolescence, for instance, may end at the age of 13 or 14, or not until the mid-twenties. Old schemata tend to be static and to emphasize either the abilities characteristic of various stages or the social and moral responsibilities of particular phases. Contemporary theories are more dynamic: they stress changes in man's psychological tasks, development in his personality and shifts in his private goals.

One of the oldest life schemes on record is set forth in the Talmud, that great book of early Jewish civil and religious law. It outlines 14 stages, emphasizing the religious and social obligations of the earlier ones and the biological characteristics of the later ones. "At five years," the Talmud advises, "the age is reached for the study of Scripture; at ten for the study of Mishnah [the Talmudic tenets]; at thirteen for the fulfillment of the Commandments; at fifteen for the study of the Talmud; at eighteen for marriage; at twenty for seeking a livelihood; at thirty for entering into one's full strength; at forty for understanding; at fifty for counsel; at sixty a man attains old age; at seventy the hoary head; at eighty the gift of special strength; at ninety he bends beneath the weight of his years; at a hundred he is as if he were already dead and had passed away from the world."

Of all the ancient analyses, the most modern, in a sense, is that of Confucius. In the Sixth Century B.C., the Chinese philosopher set down a scheme that was highly sophisticated in its emphasis on psychological development during the adult years. "At fifteen I set my heart upon learning," the Confucian *Analects* say. "At thirty, I had planted my feet firm upon the ground. At forty, I no longer suffered from perplexities. At fifty, I knew what were the biddings of heaven. At sixty, I heard them with docile ear. At seventy, I could follow the dictates of my own heart; for what I desired no longer overstepped the boundaries of right."

Somewhat later and half a world away, Plato offered a view of the adult years based on learning ability in early life and the obligation for public service in later years. Qualified adults should study until they were 30 years old, the exceptionally gifted until 35, Plato advised. After 50, he said, these two elite groups should dedicate the rest of their lives to science and to running the government. The Romans separated the adult years into four segments—adolescence, youth, virility and senescence—with the chief though not the sole emphasis on biological characteristics at each of these phases.

The most famous of all life-cycle descriptions is Shakespeare's in *As You Like It*. John Clausen analyzes it in the light of contemporary views about the life span: "Of Shakespeare's seven ages, the first two and the last two are specifically age-linked: 'At first the infant, muling and puking in the nurse's arms; then the whining schoolboy,' and, at the other end, 'the sixth age shifts into the lean and slippered pantaloon, with spectacles on nose and pouch on side . . . ' and finally 'last scene of all . . . is second childishness and mere oblivion.' The other three 'ages' are really social roles—lover, soldier, justice—that have a strong age reference, especially if one considers each as a kind of ideal type. Romeo, the lover, is strictly an adolescent; the soldier, 'full of strange oaths,' is *par excellence* the young adult male; and the lawyer does not often become a justice until he has acquired the wisdom and the round belly of middle age." As Clausen sees it, "Shakespeare's seven ages are a dramatic statement of the fact that persons change markedly from one age level to the next in the images they evoke and in the selves they present to the world."

As behavioral experts began to study the life cycle scientifically, they soon found that they had set themselves an extremely difficult task. To be certain that findings about one group of people apply to others, a large and varied sample must be observed, yet no one researcher can examine so many lives so very closely. For one thing, a middle-aged investigator starting to follow the lives of a group of young people is likely to retire, or die, long before his subjects have come anywhere near the end of their own life cycles. But more important are the va-

Global life expectancy

There are young countries, middle-aged ones and elderly ones. The youthful crowd in Subiaco, Italy *(below)*, reflects the fact that three fifths of all Italians are under 40. But Pakistan, where birth control is rare and life expectancy short, is the youngest; United Nations age profiles of the most populous nations prove it has the highest percentage of people under 20 *(right)*.

Japan has the highest proportion of inhabitants between 20 and 39, reflecting the baby boom after World War II. West Germany is a paradox. It has a large number of people under 20, but proportionally they are few: the country's high life expectancy and low birth rate give it the highest percentage of over-60-year-olds among the countries that were surveyed.

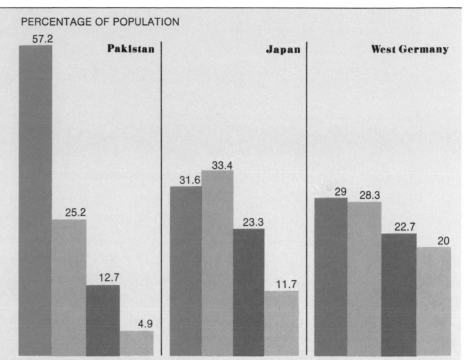

PERCENTAGE OF POPULATION

Pakistan

57.2 (0-19), 25.2 (20-39), 12.7 (40-59), 4.9 (over 60)

Japan

31.6 (0-19), 33.4 (20-39), 23.3 (40-59), 11.7 (over 60)

West Germany

29 (0-19), 28.3 (20-39), 22.7 (40-59), 20 (over 60)

Age: 0-19, 20-39, 40-59, over 60

garics of human nature: the same facts in a person's life look different at different points in the life cycle.

Psychiatrist George Vaillant, one of the few who has done extensive research into the life cycle, tells of a subject named Jordan who, at the age of 19, told an interviewer that on perhaps 40 occasions he had had the same dream. It was about two trees growing together and meeting at the top, presumably a disguised representation of sexual intercourse. Another fact the young man reported was that he was currently going to Mass four times a week.

However, 30 years later and still under study, the same individual told his interviewer that (1) the only childhood dream he could remember was of himself urinating behind a garage and that (2) he had become skeptical about religion just as soon as he entered college. "Once 49, Mr. Jordan no longer remembered correctly what had happened at 19; both a dream repeated 40 times and church-going repeated four times a week were forgotten," Vaillant said, and offered an explanation in metaphor, "It is common for caterpillars to become butterflies and then to maintain that in their youth they had been little butterflies. Maturation makes liars of us all."

Sigmund Freud is one of the precursors of contemporary life-cycle theorists. Psychoanalysis as he developed it emphasized early psychological growth progressing through several childhood stages, and it held that personality and patterns of behavior were in most cases fairly well set by adolescence. Freud believed that major changes were not the rule in adulthood, but he recognized that they occur in some people; his treatment produced them in many adults. Moreover, he once wrote that "The aim of all life is death," implying, as Karl Groffman notes, that the developmental theory of psychoanalysis could very well be extended to the entire life span. Some of Freud's successors, among them Lidz, have done just that.

The true spiritual father of life-cycle theory and of modern adult developmental psychology is Carl Gustav Jung, who began as a disciple of Freud but eventually broke away to formulate his own brand of psychoanalysis. To Jung, it was ridiculous to believe that growth is finished and maturity reached by the end of adolescence; in his view, development continued as long as life itself.

Jungian theory holds that the life cycle is made up of two stages. The first lasts until about the age of 40. In the years up to then, the individual comes to terms with the outer world, and his ego, the part of the personality that deals with external reality, is formed. The most important task of this period, Jung thought, is for the individual to divest himself of the last remnants of childishness by finding lasting solutions to early childhood conflicts that, in most people, still linger on even when adolescence is over.

Life's second stage, said Jung, is devoted to a process of inner growth and development called individuation. The aim of the process is self-realization—a goal that can be approached but never fully realized. In this phase of adulthood, a person's task is to discover his real self and to strive for unification of ideas and outlook. In addition, he must confront and try to understand what Jung called the collective unconscious, a sphere that lies even deeper than the individual's personal unconscious and contains, Jung believed, "the wisdom and experience of uncounted centuries."

Although Jung theorized about the life span and investigated it while treating his patients, he made no systematic studies. The first formal research to produce meaningful results was done by a group of Austrian psychologists headed by Charlotte Bühler. During the '20s and '30s they analyzed 400 life spans—including those of such diverse people as Goethe's mother, doctors, lawyers, janitors and the unemployed. Bühler and her associates questioned living people and used written material, including diaries, letters and biographies, to learn about the rest.

Analyzing the data, Bühler and her colleagues divided their subjects' lives into five periods. The first was of course childhood. The second began somewhere between the ages of 16 and 20 and, not surprisingly, was marked by an "expansion of the dimensions," that is, an increasing number of different activities, many of them preparations for the remainder of the adult years. The third phase, the only one to which Bühler gave a special name, was called the culmination period and began ordinarily between the ages of 26 and 30. This was the most active and fruitful stage.

Bühler discovered that very often the fourth phase was ushered in with a psychological crisis at about the age of 50. At this point many people exhibited discontent and a new restlessness; they frequently took trips for rest and recuperation, and sometimes they changed their place of residence. Most subjects in this phase of the study felt the death of friends and relatives more keenly than they had in earlier years of their lives, when it was easier to form new relationships. As physical strength and energy slackened, people in phase four often changed their vocations: one sailor became a writer, an actor turned director and an athlete switched to the role of trainer.

Interestingly enough, the early years of the fifth period, which began at about the age of 64, were very similar to the second period in some ways: in both of these stages, men and women began making plans for the future. In old age, Bühler found, most men and women fell into one of four groups. Some felt that they had accomplished what they wanted to and were content to sit back and relax. Others "felt that their active life was never finished and . . . continued striving to the end." A third group was dissatisfied but, lacking the physical or psychological strength to keep trying, found "an unhappy sort of resignation." In the last category were those unfortunate ones who had "led thoughtless and meaningless lives" and, in the final phase of their existence, experienced feelings of frustration, guilt and regret.

Bühler's work may have led the way, but the most thought-provoking and most influential theorist has been Erik Erikson, the remarkable Danish-born psychoanalyst. A Freudian who went beyond Freud, Erikson concluded that personality development does not end with puberty but continues throughout adulthood. He accepted Freud's basic hypothesis—that human beings go through six psychosexual phases of growth: oral, anal, genital, oedipal, latent and pubescent. But Erikson established that there are also eight psychosocial stages during which growth is based not on sexual instincts but on the relationship between the individual and the world he lives in.

Each of Erikson's stages brings its own crisis, "a turning point for better or for worse, a crucial period in which a decisive turn one way or another is unavoidable." The choice is always between the two distinctive components, one positive and one negative, that belong to each of the phases in the life cycle.

Erikson defined four childhood stages, in which the choices are trust versus mistrust, autonomy versus doubt, initiative versus guilt and industry versus inferiority. Whether or not the positive component outweighs the negative at the end of each phase depends very much on the child's relationship with the crucial figures in his life: his parents, teachers, brothers and sisters, and friends. If these people give a child reason to trust the world, to rely on himself, to dare new activities and to make and do practical things, then he will develop the virtues of hope, will, purpose and competence.

Erikson's fifth stage is adolescence, in which the choice is identity versus role confusion. The conflict centers on the young person's sense of certainty—or uncertainty—about who he is. The virtue that develops during this period is fidelity, by which Erikson means "the ability to sustain loyalties freely pledged." Erikson's notion of identity, the concept for which he is best known, developed after he had studied two very different groups of people, American Indians and World War II veterans. When Erikson worked with the Oglala Sioux of Pine Ridge, South Dakota, and with the Yurok of northern California, he found many young men were suffering from disturbances that he could not explain by conventional psychoanalytic theories of sexual development. These youths felt uprooted from their Indian culture, yet they had no sense of belonging to the white world either. This malaise turned out to be quite similar to a condition Erikson noted among men of quite different racial and cultural backgrounds. While working at a rehabilitation center in San Francisco, he treated World War II veterans who were troubled because they could not reconcile what they had felt and done during the war with their prewar ideals. Neither the Indians nor the veterans could determine just what kinds of people they were or ought to be; they were suffering from "role confusion," or "identity confusion."

Explorers of the human span

"Our civilization really does not harbor a concept of the whole of life, as do the civilizations of the East," Erik Erikson once wrote. Western experts in human behavior are now trying to remedy this lack. Shown here are five pioneers in the effort to interpret human development through the life cycle. All but one are Americans, reflecting the fact that systematic life-cycle studies have centered in the United States.

Swiss psychoanalyst Carl Gustav Jung can be called the father of life-cycle psychology in the West. Jung disagreed with Freud's emphasis on childhood as the decision period of development. He held that personality develops throughout life as the individual learns to integrate the outer world of reality with the inner realm of fantasy. Jung called this maturing process individuation, "the evolution of the psyche to its wholeness."

Most influential of life-cycle theorists, psychoanalyst Erik H. Erikson concluded that crisis is the key to development. He wrote of growth in terms of "the conflicts, inner and outer, which the vital personality weathers, reemerging from each crisis with an increased sense of inner unity, with an increase of good judgment, and an increase in the capacity 'to do well' according to his own standards and to the standards of those who are significant to him."

Some years later, Erikson clarified his conception of identity by quoting a letter that psychologist William James once wrote to his wife: "A man's character is discernible in the mental or moral attitude in which, when it came upon him, he felt himself most deeply and intensely active and alive. At such moments there is a voice inside which speaks and says: '*This* is the real me!'"

Very often, Erikson warned, the young adolescent does not succeed in developing this kind of positive identity because he has a negative identity thrust upon him from outside, or he chooses the negative identity vindictively to get back at someone who has treated him badly.

Psychologist David Elkind, expounding on Erikson's views, cited the poignant case of a 16-year-old girl who was arrested for prostitution near a military base. The girl had begun dressing provocatively and going out with boys at the age of 12—at her mother's urging. When she came home from dates, her unhappy mother satisfied her own frustrat-

Psychiatrist Roger L. Gould began to study the life span after his clinical work showed him that people of similar ages have similar problems. "The evolution of a personality continues through the fifth decade of life," he wrote. "A person does not possess the full range of his uniqueness after merely passing through adolescence.... The process of formation continues through stages of life that we are just beginning to recognize."

Daniel J. Levinson, a social psychologist at Yale, began by investigating middle life, then turned to other periods. "No one's life is fully integrated," says Levinson, "and it is never entirely static. It changes over time, but the changes are not capricious. The individual's life has a structure that evolves over time." Levinson's special interest is in exploring how individuals and societies "create living conditions that foster development in adulthood."

Bernice Neugarten studied thousands of men and women of all ages. A social psychologist at the University of Chicago, Neugarten points out that, with the possible exception of Erikson's major contributions, "There is no integrated body of theory that encompasses the total life span." She also notes the difficulty of proving what appears to be true about the life cycle: "Much more is known than can be easily demonstrated."

ed sexual impulses vicariously by demanding, as Elkind said, "a kiss-by-kiss, caress-by-caress description of the evening's activities"—and then she called her daughter a "whore" and a "dirty tramp." After she had been arrested, the girl told Elkind, "Hell, I have the name, so I might as well play the role."

Erikson's sixth stage is young adulthood, when the conflict is intimacy versus isolation. The virtue to be developed is love, defined as "mutuality of devotion forever subduing the antagonisms inherent in divided functions." Intimacy, in Erikson's sense of emotional closeness, may develop between friends: soldiers who face the terrible dangers of battle together are often genuinely committed to each other. Usually, intimacy occurs between husbands and wives, but marriage does not guarantee closeness. As Erikson said, "There are partnerships which amount to an isolation à deux."

In such partnerships husbands and wives cannot successfully resolve the crisis of stage seven, generativity—a concern for future generations versus self-absorption, the turning inward that shuts out the rest of the world. Erikson warned that "the mere fact of having or even wanting children does not achieve generativity." To his mind, true generativity calls for a great deal more than such basics as feeding children, sheltering them, buying them clothes and sending them to school. It also requires a deep involvement in the welfare of future generations and concern for the kind of society in which they will live, as well as a genuine attempt to give back to the world what the individual has taken from it. Unless generativity can be achieved, neither husband nor wife is likely to develop the stage seven virtue of care—a person's "love for his works and ideas as well as for his children."

In old age, the last of Erikson's eight stages, the issue is integrity versus despair, and the virtue that emerges when all goes well is wisdom, which Erikson defined as "detached concern with life itself, in the face of death itself." When an old person can look back on his life with satisfaction, he experiences a sense of integrity, and death seems almost acceptable. By contrast, an elderly person despairs when he feels he has missed important opportunities and when he must face the inevitable fact that it is too late to start afresh.

As Erikson defined it, however, there is much more to integrity than that: "It is the acceptance of one's one and only life cycle . . . as something that had to be and that, by necessity, permitted of no substitutions. It thus means a new and different love of one's parents, free of the wish that they should have been different, and an acceptance of the fact that one's life is one's own responsibility. It is a sense of comradeship with men and women of distant times and of different pursuits who have created orders and objects and sayings conveying human dignity and love."

One of the most striking examples of Erikson's concept of late-life integrity is a man whom Erikson never met or treated, a man who probably had never read any of Erikson's books. This man's name was Ed Hart, and he was one of 435 subjects in a study of old age by anthropologists Margaret Clark and Barbara Anderson. Hart was 93 years old when he was interviewed, and by then he had outlived three wives and two sons and had survived a business failure, a nervous breakdown, several operations and near blindness. Yet his identity was intact. "He is first, last and always himself," the researchers said. "This man made a profound impression on all our interviewers. They found him alert, intelligent, serene and wise. His self-acceptance is complete. He found it difficult to describe himself in terms of the list of various personality traits we submitted to him; he simply stated, more appropriately, 'I'm Ed Hart and I don't want to be anyone else—I will be the same ten years from now, if I'm alive!' "

After Erikson published his first book about the life cycle in 1950, several investigators began to make detailed studies of adulthood by interviewing men and women about their experiences and emotions and then looking for patterns common to many lives. Among the investigations sweeping most broadly across several periods of life are those by social psychologist Daniel Levinson of Yale, psychiatrist Roger Gould of the University of California at Los Angeles and psychologist Bernice Neugarten at the University of Chicago. Nothing that they have found contradicts Erikson's theories; much supports them. These investigators have now documented the change, growth and development that continue throughout the life span.

Daniel Levinson's particular interest was initially the time of life around the age of 40. In the late 1960s, he and his colleagues began an intensive study of 40 men aged 35 to 45. The subjects were a special and diverse group, evenly divided among industrial workers (both blue-collar and white-collar), business executives, academic biologists and novelists. After many hours of probing with psychological personality tests and interviews, Levinson discovered that he would not be able to understand middle life unless he knew what had gone before, and his interest widened to encompass the whole life span.

Levinson's approach is a broad one. Some theorists focus on personality development in adulthood, studying changes in psychological

One woman's graceful, self-confident passage through the adult years is recorded in photographs of Anna Ludmila Grabowicz at the ages

of 23, 35, 42, 66, 75 and 90 (left to right, insets top to bottom). A Ukrainian lawyer's wife, she came to the United States at 75 and lived to 99.

characteristics such as motives, values and attitudes. Others focus more on career development or on changes in social behavior and roles. Levinson seeks to encompass both approaches. His developmental periods involve changes in what he calls the individual life structure—the overall pattern or design of the person's life.

The life structure includes participation in society—the groups or institutions an individual belongs to, and his roles within them—as well as the personal meanings they have for him and the aspects of himself that are expressed or excluded. Levinson hypothesizes that adult development involves an alternation between periods of transition and periods of stability. In the transitional periods, the life structure undergoes major change; in the periods of greater stability, the life structure is more securely established, and one pursues his external goals and personal fulfillment within it.

The life cycle as Levinson conceives it is a sequence of five major eras, each lasting about 20 years. The first era, pre-adulthood, extends from birth to roughly the age of 20. Then follow early adulthood (20 to 40), middle adulthood (40 to 60), late adulthood (60 to 80) and late, late adulthood (beyond 80). The character of life changes from one era to the next. There is a series of developmental periods within each era, and a period of transition (ordinarily lasting some four to five years) links and overlaps adjacent eras. Levinson's eras, he explained, "do not form a hierarchical progression from lower to higher levels; one period is not intrinsically better or more advanced than the preceding ones." Instead, they are like the seasons of the year: "Each season has its own tasks, character and outcome . . . all are essential to the full cycle of nature."

To Levinson, the transition at the age of 30 is especially important. During this period, each of the men Levinson studied examined his own progress so far and considered whether or not he wanted to change his life course. Sometimes the period was bewildering. "It was like being in the middle of the ocean with no life preserver; I didn't know which way I was going to go," one subject remembered. In other cases the transition went more smoothly. For example, Frank M. was a vice president in electronics by the age of 32 and had already amassed a fortune of more than a million dollars. He was on the way up in the corporate structure, yet he decided to risk what he had achieved in the hope of winning even more in the end: he founded a corporation of his own, started a new life and made up his mind that he would become the giant of his industry in another 10 years.

Levinson found that the midlife transition, which lasts roughly from

40 to 45 years of age, is a bridging period between early adulthood and middle adulthood. This period involves both the end of youth and the initiation of middle age. The individual's primary task is to draw selectively upon the past, to develop more fully his inner resources and to form the basis for a new life structure in middle age. This bridging time also offers the individual a fresh opportunity to grow up and to deal with the little boy that still exists inside the middle-aged man. "But that little boy doesn't give up so easily," Levinson commented. During this transition period a man "is very touchy about others controlling him and containing him. He is more likely to regard his boss or his colleagues as oppressing him or his wife as either too demanding or too dependent. He often acts very peculiarly then. People say, 'What's got into him?' "

Anxiety is a dominant motif at this stage of life, Levinson said. "People would like to believe that life begins at 40, but the great fear is that it ends there." At middle life the problem is to steer a course between worrying about growing old and trying futilely to stay young, Levinson

Reversing the life cycle, the aged and decrepit in this 1546 painting by Lucas Cranach the Elder arrive by wheelbarrow, on litters and in heavily laden carts to bathe in the Fountain of Youth, and to be miraculously rejuvenated into frolicking young adults.

noted. "It is terrifying to live one's middle age in the shadow of death, and it is a self-defeating illusion to live it in the shadow of youth, or as though one were still simply young. The key developmental task of middle age is to outgrow some of the immaturities and illusions of youth and build a fuller, more balanced life."

A more extensive, less personalized, investigation of adult change has been made by Roger Gould. He studied 524 middle-class men and women ranging in age from 16 to 60. He gave each person a list of 128 statements and questions, some dealing with relationships to family and friends, others exploring the subjects' feelings about time, and still others probing personalities, jobs and sexual behavior. The subjects were asked to rank each item on the list for its importance in their personal lives. (Some details of the results are presented in graph form on pages 41, 69 and 103.)

Gould found that the rankings changed as his subjects grew older, reflecting the trends noted by Levinson. "The direction of change," said Gould, "is toward becoming more tolerant of oneself." In the earliest years, children imagine adults to be perfect, and as they grow up they often try to hold themselves to standards no human being could meet. As Gould put it, "A child's idealized image of an adult can become the adult's painful measure of himself."

Gould found the twenties marked by confidence and optimism. In this period, adults "felt that they were the now generation," that "now was the time to live, and now was the time to build for the future, both professionally and personally." The thirties were more self-reflective; people questioned what they were doing and why.

Gould discovered that the forties brought awareness that time is finite, as well as "reconciliation of what is with what might have been." Many of the men and women in their forties gave high ranking to the statement, "I try to be satisfied with what I have and not to think so much about the things I probably won't be able to get." In the fifties, self-acceptance was even greater. At the same time, Gould said, his subjects "were more eager to have 'human' experiences, such as sharing the joys, sorrows, confusions and triumphs of everyday life rather than searching for the glamor, the glitter, the power or the abstract." Taken together, these stages might well seem to be a prescription for living. They are not, Gould emphasizes. No one, he warned, should try to alter his own life to fit them; many successful, happy people do not match the research findings.

What is probably the largest examination of adult life is the one that Bernice Neugarten began in the 1950s. Over the years she and her colleagues have made some 80 separate studies, cross-examining thousands of men and women in cities, towns and villages through interviews and written questionnaires that probe for personality changes at various stages of life.

Neugarten found middle age to be a major turning point, and she observed that the period has both painful and gratifying aspects. The middle-aged become poignantly aware that they are no longer young. She quotes a journalist who summarized the feelings of many of her subjects. "The realization suddenly struck me that I had become, perhaps not an old fogy but surely a middle-aged fogy, for the train was filled with college boys returning from vacation. They cruised up and down the aisles, boisterous, but not obnoxious. Yet most of the adult passengers were annoyed with them, including myself. I sat there, feeling a little like Eliot's Prufrock, 'so meticulously composed, buttoned-up, bespectacled, mouth thinly set.' Squaresville."

Yet many of the middle-aged men and women Neugarten talked to felt that they were more fully in charge of their lives than they ever had been before. Some even thought themselves better off than their younger co-workers. One remarked, "I know now exactly what I can do best, and how to make the best use of my time. I know how to delegate authority, but also what decisions to make myself. I know how to buffer myself from troublesome people. It takes time to learn how to cut through the red tape and how to get the organization to work for me. All this is what makes the difference between me and a young man, and it's all this that gives me the advantage."

For some of Neugarten's middle-aged subjects, the realization of advancing age became an incentive to further accomplishment. "Time is now a two-edged sword," said one. "To some of my friends, it acts as a prod; to others a brake. It adds a certain anxiety, but I must say it adds a certain zest in seeing how much pleasure can still be obtained, how many good years one can still arrange, how many new activities can be undertaken."

Most theorists emphasize that although life stages follow one another in unvarying order, they are not tied to particular ages; that is, the psychology of the life cycle depends not only on biology but on society too. One of the most important factors determining when stages begin and how long they last is social class, Neugarten observed.

In one of her investigations, she studied hundreds of adults aged 40 to 70 who lived in a small city, asking such questions as "What would you call the periods of life that people go through after they are grown up?" and "At what age does each period begin, for most people?" The typical upper-middle-class business executive or professional thought that a man is most likely to be settled at the age of 30, that he becomes mature, is in his prime and has the most confidence in himself when he is 40, and that he reaches middle age only at 50, old age not before 70. However, for the unskilled worker in Neugarten's sample, life moved faster: he considered a man settled by the age of 25, already middle-aged at 40 and old by 60.

Culture has an even more profound effect than class. In societies that can provide only primitive health care and poor food, age distributions are radically different. So many babies die at birth that to maintain even a steady population young women must bear numerous children; women who are preoccupied with bearing and nursing infants over their fertile years have few if any of the choices that are available to young adults elsewhere.

Similar cultural restrictions apply to young men. If the way of life is simple—depending entirely on unsophisticated occupations that demand no long years of formal education—the periods of adolescence and young adulthood blend. An adolescent takes on men's work—the kind is ordained by the culture—and may be accorded adult responsibilities and freedoms early in his teens; in technologically advanced societies he will still be a dependent schoolboy and, if he were to become a physician or university scholar, might remain in this adolescent stage until his late twenties.

Since simple cultures offer few opportunities for later change, mid-life is barely distinguishable as a separate adult period. And so few people survive to old age that the meaning of this stage too is totally different from its aspect in more complex cultures. The elderly present no problems to society or to their families; quite the contrary, they are treasured like other rare and valuable individuals.

Societies also shape the life cycle by encouraging, or prohibiting, certain kinds of behavior at certain times. The most obvious effect is that produced by differing attitudes toward sexual activity. Many cultures —advanced as well as primitive ones—tolerate or approve sexual experimentation among adolescents. Such freedom eliminates a major source of stress during this stage, and, in the opinion of many scientists, greatly reduces the turmoil associated with growing up in more puritanical societies.

Social influences become especially marked in old age, making this phase of the life cycle quite different in the East and the West. In the East, Buddhism dictates respect for older people; in the West, the elderly are often seen as washed up, useless and burdensome. Carl Jung deplored this difference and pleaded for its elimination: "The afternoon of human life cannot be merely a pitiful appendage to life's morning. In primitive tribes we observe that the old people are almost always the guardians of the mysteries and the laws, and it is in these that the cultural heritage of the tribe is expressed. How does the matter stand with us? Where is the wisdom of our old people, where are their precious secrets and their visions?"

The old belief, Roger Gould observed, was that "while children change, adults only age." Now the experts know that adults grow too, and that not only childhood but every time in the life cycle is important because it is part of and contributes to human development. Each phase is in fact dependent on the ones that went before; an old person cannot achieve ego integrity in Erikson's sense unless he earlier achieved some degree of trust, autonomy, initiative, industry, identity, intimacy and generativity.

There is also a bright side to this continuing challenge. Personality is not necessarily fixed forever by childhood experience. "Even though development is impeded or altered," said Theodore Lidz, "compensations are possible, and deficiencies can even be turned into strengths." Life offers not just a second chance, but many chances; unhappy choices at critical turning points in the life cycle are not irrevocable. Since the same problems crop up throughout the adult years, fresh solutions can be found and new successes can overcome old failures.

Whether the life cycle unfolds without too much hindrance, or seems to go awry but is later set right, the final years of adulthood can be nearly as dynamic, psychologically, as the earlier ones. The life of the late Supreme Court Justice Oliver Wendell Holmes Jr. proves as much. On his 90th birthday, Holmes told admirers: "The riders in a race do not stop short when they reach the goal. There is a little finishing canter before coming to a standstill. There is time to hear the kind voice of friends and to say to one's self: 'The work is done.' But just as one says that, the answer comes: 'The race is over, but the work never is done while the power to work remains.' " Then Holmes underlined his philosophy with a quotation from a Fifth Century Latin poet: "Death plucks my ear and says, 'Live—I am coming.' "

Marking the milestones

In every society, rituals and ceremonies mark life's major milestones and dramatize the changing status of the individual as he makes his way from the cradle to the grave. They are visible signals to the community that one stage of life has been left behind and another one has begun.

The form of these observances may be as simple as an oath of allegiance in a recruiting office or as elaborate as a Hindu wedding with elephants, sacred ceremonial fires and huge trays of delicately prepared foods. In traditional societies the major transitions—birth, puberty, marriage, childbearing and death—are marked by formal ceremonies known to anthropologists as rites of passage. These observances often entail periods of fasting or isolation, and physical ordeals.

Western societies observe some of the transitions from stage to stage more casually because the stages are not so clearly defined. The entry into adulthood is marked by a series of ceremonies large and small—the issuance of a driver's license, the granting of a university diploma, a coming-out party. However, there are some stages of Western life unknown elsewhere—retirement from a job is one—and they have given rise to rites peculiar to industrialized society.

The dearth of formalized ritual in the West is a handicap, in the opinion of many social scientists who believe that the rigid observances in older societies serve a useful purpose. By telling the individual exactly where he is in the life cycle and what is expected of him, they give him a clear sense of his own role and his own identity—a sense often lacking among Western peoples.

While a chief's wife gives birth, sorcerers of Africa's Ivory Coast honor a baby's entry into life and his mother's entry into parenthood with a ritual. They toss a hypnotized child while wielding a knife to symbolize opening the womb.

At a Bar Mitzvah ceremony, a young Jewish boy, wearing a man's prayer shawl for the first time, chants in ancient Hebrew. This key rite of passage signifies the admission of boys at the age of 13 into the adult religious community.

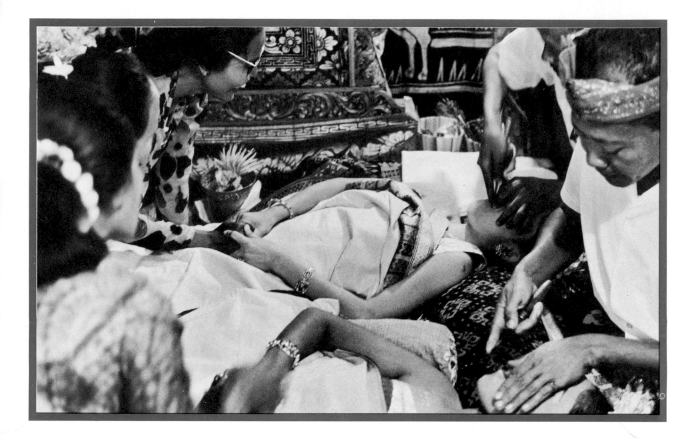

Wrapped in white cloth, Balinese girls undergo a rite that requires their upper teeth to be filed down—a protection, it is believed, against evil qualities. Puberty rites in traditional societies frequently entail physical marking, such as teeth filing, face scarring, or genital mutilation.

Led around her village in central Brazil by two young men blowing on bamboo pipes, a young Camayura girl completes a three-year-long puberty rite. During this period, which followed her first menstruation, she has been kept in seclusion and taught cooking and other domestic skills she will need as a wife.

The threshold of adulthood

Puberty, the biological coming of age, is observed as a social coming of age in many religious communities and traditional societies. These rites of passage begin the preparation of boys and girls for adult responsibilities. So important is this preparation that in some primitive cultures puberty rites have evolved around a theme of death and resurrection. Thus, a child may be isolated or taken away from his village for days or weeks, when he is said to be dead. Upon his return he is considered reborn, ready to become an adult.

The responsibilities of maturity

Rites conferring adult status vary from culture to culture, but the impact is always the same. They identify individuals as fully independent, responsible citizens. Thus a ritual haircut inducts a Masai warrior *(right)* into the tribal council, and voting makes an 18-year-old American *(below)* part of the political process in his society.

In traditional cultures single events such as marriage or childbirth often determine adulthood. Many Western nations, however, accord adult status in stages—a driver's license in mid-teens, a coming-out party at about 16 and legal majority a few years later.

Seated with his heavily veiled bride in a marriage booth, a young Hindu attains adulthood by wedding. Adult status is denied his wife until she has a child.

Preparing to cast her first ballot, an 18-year-old North Carolina girl is given instructions. Lowering the U.S. voting age in 1971 reduced the age at which adult privileges were granted in many states.

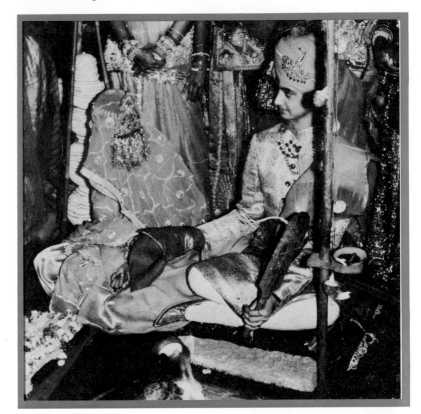

A ritual haircut by his mother makes
this young Masai warrior a full-fledged
adult. He will now belong to the
tribal council that governs his people.

The end of a working career

Although people everywhere retire—
that is, relinquish their roles as directly productive members of the working community—only in Western and
Westernized societies is the retirement
ceremony observed as a rite of passage.
An aging Hindu in India may renounce
his material possessions and leave his
family to become a wandering holy
man. Among the Ainu in Japan, elders
assume ritual responsibilities for the society. But only in industrialized societies does a ritual mark the change from
a working to a nonworking status. The
ceremony has quickly become institu-
tionalized with certain traditional trap-
pings: a banquet concluding with sen-
timental speeches and the award of a
gold watch or other token marks one of
life's most abrupt and, in some cases,
most upsetting changes.

At a retirement dinner in New York,
an executive of Coats and Clark, a sewing
supplies company, presents printing
production manager Kenneth Bohlen with
a going-away check as the retiring
employee's wife and co-workers look on.
The ceremony brought to a close
a 27-year association with the firm.

Balinese villagers watch the cremation of an aged aristocrat in his flamboyantly decorated, bull-shaped sarcophagus. Funerals are joyous events in Bali: destroying the body, it is believed, frees the soul to ascend to heaven where it awaits rebirth as a nobler being.

Gathering for the final ceremonial

Ceremonies surrounding death are the most deeply felt and often the most elaborate rites in the life cycle. Such rituals help surviving members of the family adjust to the shock of their loss and also to the new roles they must assume.

At a wake for the head of an Irish household, for example, the body lies in an open casket in the home for two days—its presence in such familiar surroundings reinforcing the reality of the death. The loss is mourned with intense emotional outbursts that enable survivors to express their grief. At the same time, the presence of many friends and relatives confirms the new roles of the widow and of the son who will assume his father's responsibilities.

A mournful procession in southern Spain makes its way to the graveyard, led by priests whose umbrellas shelter them from a gray spring rain. Women of rural Spain continue observances for the dead long after interment, cleaning and decorating tombs on All Saints Day.

A Window on Adulthood

"Scrubs had maneuvered through his daughter's adolescence like a marine moving through a mined field." This portrait of an embattled parent, written by the humorist Russell Baker, who had safely maneuvered himself through the adolescences of a daughter and two sons, suggests the explosive potential of the entrance into the adult years. For this period can be the most volatile and difficult stretch of life, a time that is laden with the possibility of disaster and yet holds the brightest promise for the future.

It is a time of paradoxes—torturous ecstasy that caused Shakespeare to write, "I would there were no age between sixteen and three-and-twenty," as well as agony that led a modern British psychoanalyst to lament that the only cure is "five years." It revolves around a not-quite child, not-quite grownup, as self-centered as the girl preoccupied with her music at left, engaged in a fateful search for an individual place in the world. The landscape of these years is dotted with emotional peaks and valleys whose heights and depths will probably never be matched later. These obstacles confront the youth of every culture. They are traversed most readily in traditional societies, where centuries of experience have defined clear paths for the transition from childhood into adult responsibility. But in modern technological cultures, buffeted and bewildered by rapid change, the turmoil and confusion suggested by Russell Baker are acute. There adolescence often gives rise to behavior that defies explanation, and yet is a natural part of the healthy individual's development.

"Actions and attitudes which in an adult would be considered symptomatic of severe emotional disturbance are now understood to be a normal part of that tumultuous period of life marking the transitional stage between childhood and adulthood known as adolescence," explained Graham Blaine Jr., a psychiatrist at Harvard and Radcliffe. "Rebellious and provocative behavior, isolation and withdrawal, extreme lethargy and apathy, peculiar ways of dressing, a bizarre and unintelligible language, strange obsessions and fads—all these are characteristics which would be considered signs of illness in an adult, but they can now be accepted, albeit somewhat reluctantly and woefully, by parents as growing pains in teen-age sons and daughters. They are not cause for alarm."

Underlying this strange behavior are the profound physical and psychological changes of adolescence, triggered by sexual maturation, or puberty. It includes a whole sequence of biological developments. The most important is, of course, the growth of the sex organs and the tremendous upsurge in sexual impulses, which are more powerful during adolescence than at any other stage of life. There is no fixed time for the start of puberty. Girls, who mature about two years earlier than boys, now generally begin to menstruate between 10 and 16. But the average age of puberty has been declining steadily and markedly at least since the Industrial Revolution. Records from the early 19th Century indicate that girls then matured at 15 1/2. Over the past century puberty has come to both sexes about four months earlier every decade. Nutrition is a major influence: well-nourished Western girls have their first menstrual period just before the age of 13, compared to 15 1/2 among poverty-ridden Bantu in the South African Transkei.

In girls the first sign of puberty is generally breast "budding," a hint of development that is not yet voluptuous enough to justify a bra. The next change is the appearance of pubic hair. Padding begins to appear in the right places; and there is a rapid and dramatic spurt in height. Menstruation then occurs. However, ovulation may not take place for 12 to 18 months.

In boys, puberty usually begins with enlargement of the testes. Pubic hair appears next, after which the penis gets bigger and the voice breaks as the larynx enlarges. The next landmark is the first ejaculation. Before long the muscles begin to develop rapidly and the boy shoots up, gaining an average of four or five inches in height a year compared to two inches annually during childhood. His trunk lengthens more than his legs and over a longer period; he keeps needing new, longer jackets for a year after he stops outgrowing his trousers. At this stage, the boy loses a lot of fat, so that he acquires a gangly, coltish look. Before long he is examining the down on his face in the mirror, and shaving whether he needs to or not.

What makes life so stressful and upsetting for the modern adolescent is that he has four difficult tasks to accomplish. He must deal with his awakened sexuality in a world that, sexual revolution or no, is leery of sex and especially of sex for adolescents. Freud called this first task

The cares of adolescence

Adolescents can hardly wait to grow older —a feeling they share with no other age group. But another major concern of youth —their parents—reappears later in life. The feelings characteristic of adolescents (*shaded area*) emerged from a survey by psychiatrist Roger L. Gould of UCLA's School of Medicine. His team asked 524 people, ranging in age from 16 to 60, to rate a set of statements for applicability to their lives. The average ranking of each statement changed in striking patterns reflecting each age group's responses (*below and on pages 69 and 103*).

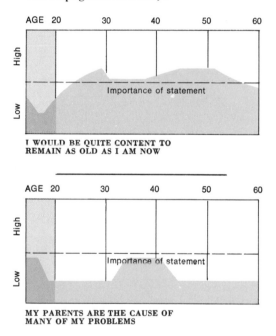

I WOULD BE QUITE CONTENT TO REMAIN AS OLD AS I AM NOW

MY PARENTS ARE THE CAUSE OF MANY OF MY PROBLEMS

achieving "genital maturity," and he saw it as the main job of adolescence. In addition the youngster must become an independent person, "not simply someone's son or daughter," as Yale psychoanalyst Theodore Lidz put it. But he must also make up his mind about what he believes in, and he must decide what social and occupational role he wants to play in life. Taken together, the four tasks add up to what psychoanalyst Erik Erikson sees as the overall problem of the adolescent: to establish a sense of identity, a feeling of certainty about who he is and where he wants to go in life. In Erikson's words, the youngster experiments to "find a niche in some section of his society, a niche which is firmly defined and yet seems to be uniquely made for him."

The first and perhaps most important of the four tasks is to cope with the urgent sexual drives of adolescence. At first these drives are directed mostly toward the parents: up to now, the child has spent most of his time with his mother and father and has naturally formed his closest ties with them. Not only his unconscious incestuous urges but all of his new sexual feelings are alarming to the young adolescent, and he guards against them in many ways. One defense is intellectualization; the youngster concentrates on thinking and studying so that he has no time or energy left over for sexual feelings or fantasies.

Another defense is asceticism; through self-denial and an austere way of life, an adolescent keeps sexuality in check. Though this strategy is most common in Europe, it is also observed in the United States. The American psychoanalyst Ira Mintz attributed the popularity of the Hare Krishna movement that began in the late 1960s in part to its usefulness as a defense. Many young adherents, he reported, showed little sexual restraint before they joined. Frightened by their own behavior, they found "in the guise of religious commitment" exactly what they needed: "a strict, ascetic society with a built-in set of controls."

One common device is the merging of drive and defense—expressing impulses, including sexual ones, while guarding against them at the same time. The endless adolescent telephone calls that are the despair of parents belong in this category. As a psychiatric study explained, "One has a voice speaking intimately into one's ear and an ear at one's lips, and yet there are no possible complications if control over sexual feelings relaxes a little."

Another kind of defense is a short-lived homosexuality, conscious or unconscious. Anne Frank, the Dutch girl who confided her typically adolescent concerns to the now-familiar diary kept while she hid from the Nazis, recorded her own transient homosexual feelings. "I remember that once when I slept with a girl friend I had a strong desire to kiss her, and that I did so . . . I asked her whether, as proof of our friendship, we should feel each other's breasts, but she refused."

When the adolescent, despite all the dodges he uses to keep from facing his new sexuality, eventually begins hesitant experiments, his first relationships are narcissistic. Concerned with himself and his own sensations, he wants only to find out what sex is like and is not much interested in his partner's feelings. Next comes the first experience of "falling in love," in which neither sex nor genuine love figure importantly. By choosing a partner rather like himself, or one with traits he would like to possess, a youngster tries to find out who he himself is or might become. "To a considerable extent," Erikson writes, "adolescent love is an attempt to arrive at a definition of one's identity by projecting one's diffused self-image on another and by seeing it thus reflected and gradually clarified. This is why so much of young love is conversation." Finally toward the end of adolescence, a youth looks for someone whose personality complements his own and makes him feel complete; in such a relationship, sex and tenderness fuse.

While moving toward this high level of sexual maturity, the young person is also striving toward the achievement of his second major goal: independence. This phase of his efforts to grow up has five major characteristics: ambivalence, moodiness, devotion to peers, rebelliousness and a distrust of adults (which is heartily reciprocated, causing the notorious generation gap).

Much of the difficulty in the struggle for independence comes from the adolescent's ambivalence. Some events of this period are both welcomed and shunned. Most boys and girls take pride in the physical signs that they are growing up. When psychologist Jerome Kagan asked girls of 15 to recall how they felt when they first menstruated, one said, "I thought I was cool," while another replied, "I started thinking that I couldn't ride my bike and couldn't do things that made me look like a baby." Both sexes are eager to tick off all the other milestones that blaze the road to adulthood in Western society: wearing make-up for the first time; earning a driver's license and owning a car; smoking cigarettes—or pot—and drinking beer; graduating from high school and then, toward the end of adolescence, going to the polls to vote. These landmarks are the modern equivalents of the rites of passage *(pages 28-37)*, or formal ceremonies, that traditionally celebrated the transition from childhood to adulthood, but they are poor substitutes because their meaning is blurred. They fail to confer an unequivocal change in status, as older rites did. Nevertheless they boost the adolescent's pride because they assure him that he is at least moving toward his destination.

Screaming and gesticulating Japanese adolescents respond ecstatically to American rock star David Cassidy at an Osaka concert. Hero worship focused on popular music figures has become commonplace among young people in many countries—a manifestation of the adolescent's search for strong personalities that serve as models in his quest for an identity of his own.

Because of the ambiguity of modern rites of passage, negotiating them can be not only difficult but also scary. One girl told Kagan that when she began to menstruate, she "started staying in on Saturdays with my mother instead of going out. I didn't want to have to think for myself." The urge to move ahead and the longing to hang back can often be observed in the same adolescent on the same day. Another young girl made a scene in the afternoon because she wanted to go out alone with a boy in his car; the same night she wanted her mother to come and tuck her into bed. A young boy wrote in an essay he composed for the Child Study Department at Vassar College, "Parents should treat boys of 15 years of age as grownups and not children"; later in the composition he wrote, "The parents should make it their job to see to it that their children do their homework."

Tina deVaron, an adolescent quoted by Kagan, wrote from the van-

Total absorption with their appearances interrupts a teen-aged couple's promenade along the boardwalk of New York City's seaside at Coney Island. This picture, taken in 1957, captures the poignant, often tormented preoccupation of young people with themselves. The narcissistic preening is in fact one of many steps toward an adolescent's achievement of a distinct personality.

tage point of age 16 about the ambivalence of her earlier adolescence: "When I was 13 or 14, I felt bereft of the time of my childhood. I knew that this time could never come back, that I would only get farther and farther away from it. I wanted to be little all over again. But at the same time I couldn't wait to be grown up; I was buying bras and eye make-up, and holding hands with boys. I can remember saying to myself, 'You are stupid to want to be big and little at the same time.' "

Most of the adolescent's ambivalence comes from his doubts, conscious or not, that he is really strong enough to go it alone. Psychiatrist Bruno Bettelheim noted that Germans sometimes call rebellious youths the *Halbstarken*, or half strong. "They feel their weakness," Bettelheim said, "but wish to deny it through a show of great strength." Even if, at moments, adolescents are willing to reveal their weakness and ask for help, they are likely to discover that they have already outgrown their parents' capacity to assist them. Tina deVaron remembers, "When I was about 12, I was very afraid of death. I didn't see the point in living if I was going to die. I used to cry and cry for my parents' attention, but they couldn't take away this fear from me; they were helpless. The strength they had had in dissolving my childhood fears was gone." In the end, she believed, their helplessness proved to be a good thing because it compelled her "to search for my understanding of me and of life, independent of my parents." Nevertheless she "felt anxious; a lonely, sick feeling would come easily."

During this period, the adolescent is engaged in a love-hate relationship with his parents. They are his models for adulthood and he admires them, but he must break away from them in order to achieve his identity. He cannot sever the cord tactfully but must slash it abruptly to prove to his parents—and to himself—that he is no longer their docile child. He may voice his defiance explicitly, in angry shouting matches. He may rebel through sullen withdrawal, or through escapades or outright delinquencies that, psychologist Kenneth Keniston maintains, are intended to embarrass parents and to announce the adolescent's emancipation. Inevitably, the teenager makes it clear that he has a low opinion of his parents' appearance and alleged accomplishments, and that he considers all their ideas hopelessly old-fashioned. "The adolescent has to criticize the parents to protect himself from an over-identification with them," psychoanalyst Irene Josselyn explained. He attacks everything his parents are, everything they stand for, because he is afraid that otherwise he will be no more than a mirror-image of one parent or the other—a reflection, instead of an individual in his own right. Parents who try to find common ground with adolescents or to keep up with their sudden, quixotic changes of direction may be in for a shock. "You find them zigging, and you try to zig, and the next thing you know you are zigging and they're zagging," commented one psychiatrist.

Because the adolescent must lose his parents psychologically, he may actually mourn for them, at least in his insecure moments. This feeling of loss helps explain the long walks he takes alone, and the tragic poetry he writes. It can also account for the new feeling of kinship with the downtrodden that he sometimes develops. In any case, the teenager's depression gives him a push toward independence, motivating him to look outside his family for satisfying relationships that make up for what he can no longer find at home.

Turning his back on his parents, the teenager naturally looks to his age mates. Indeed, adolescence is the time when the peer group can be the center of life, although this is less true in Europe than it is in the United States. The British sociologist Frank Musgrove questioned more than

Identical hair styles, modes of dress and even the same detached facial expressions are shared by teen-aged girls in a Chicago park. Conformity in appearance and behavior is paradoxically a source of both concern and reassurance to adolescents; if achieved in exactly the right degree it provides a sense of security in the struggle toward maturity.

700 adolescents and concluded that British youngsters do not feel quite the same solidarity with one another as do their American counterparts. The French historian Philippe Ariès wrote that the modern French family, including both parents and children, "digs itself in against the world." In America, by contrast, it is apparently the adolescent peer group that entrenches itself against the rest of society. Psychiatrist Daniel Offer and his fellow researchers, in their study of middle-class teenagers in Chicago, asked high school boys, "If you were alone on a desert island and you could have one person to join you, whom would you want?" A majority of the freshmen opted for a young friend of the same sex.

The peer group performs a critical function. The adolescent "finds a home away from home among his peers," said one psychiatrist. "He has the status of a big fish in a little pond. He finds all kinds of support by realizing that others are going through the same thing; they hate their parents too; they are lying about their sexual exploits and matching his fantasies, although there is much more actuality to these exploits nowadays than there used to be." The attraction of the peer group brings a desperate need to fit in. The girl who matures early feels painfully conspicuous, towering over her contemporaries, her already noticeable hips and breasts contrasting markedly with the still childish bodies of her classmates. If she has passed the crucial milestone of her first menstruation, she rightly considers herself out of step with girls who have barely entered puberty.

The young person's immersion in his peer group and his often mutinous spirit toward adult authority both contribute to the generation gap. Adults blame youth, but there is more to it than that. The generations are bound to look at the world differently because they are at different stages of the life cycle. Rapid social change also widens the generation gap. In centuries past, children could look confidently to their parents for guidance about the future because the future was certain to be about the same as the past. Nowadays things change so swiftly that young people grow up in a world their parents never knew. Margaret Mead suggested that parents who came to adulthood before World War II were pioneers in the "country of the young," a land so foreign to the experience of adults that they hardly know how to live in it themselves and certainly cannot chart it for their children.

Very often, parents unnecessarily deepen the natural gulf that separates the generations. They frequently shut off all lines of communication, and sometimes they even hate the young. Sociologist

Millard Bienvenu, who, with his colleagues, interviewed several hundred young people about their relationships with their parents, quoted a 17-year-old girl: "We rarely discuss anything important at home. We used to talk at dinner, but now that's out. Dad bought a portable TV and put it in the dining room." Parents can close off communication as well with indifference as with television sets; a cartoon portrays one teenager telling another, "My family doesn't care what I do as long as it doesn't come to their attention."

Sociologist Edgar Friedenberg speaks of the positive hatred, "usually disguised as concern," that many adults feel for adolescents. Acknowledging that it is painful to watch a youngster make what appear to be serious mistakes, Friedenberg proposes the uncomfortable idea that "at a deeper level, it may be even more painful when he does not make them, or when they turn out not to be mistakes, when he grasps and holds what eluded you, or what you dared not touch and have dreamed of ever since. . . . We may hate the young not only for getting what we never had, but for reminding us that since we never succeeded in getting it, we have no right to self-esteem."

Many children seem to be driven away from home by their parents' dislike. Teen-age runaways are a problem all over the world. In Japan special details of plainclothes policemen keep a lookout for runaways in all major cities. Close to 50,000 were picked up in 1972, and in only three fourths of the cases had the families bothered to ask the police for help in getting their youngsters back. In the United States, so many teenagers run away—an estimated one million in 1973—that social agencies have set up centers to help them in every major city and in many smaller ones. Psychiatrist Joseph Brenner, who established a medical clinic for "street people" in Cambridge, Massachusetts, told of a 19-year-old runaway who had hepatitis, was miserably depressed and wanted to go home. With her permission, Brenner telephoned the girl's well-to-do mother, who raged that she "couldn't care less" what happened to her daughter and then slammed down the receiver. Brenner waited a few minutes to give her time to cool off and then called again. "Mother's response this time was cold, measured, hostile: 'You've got her. She's yours,'" Brenner reported.

A particularly tragic case of lack of communication between parents and offspring is that of the 18-year-old daughter of a wealthy American businessman. She left school and went to New York's bohemian East Village to live in what her parents thought was "a nice hotel" with a girl "from a good family." Just five weeks later, she and a hippie boyfriend her parents had never heard of were found beaten to death in the basement of a sleazy tenement. The depth of the generation gap in the family made headlines when reporters pieced together a portrait of a young woman totally unknown to her family. Her parents described her as "a nice, outgoing, happy girl" who was shy with boys and had just enjoyed "a typical Bermuda vacation with her family," swimming, painting and shopping. On the other hand, friends in the East Village quoted the girl as saying that she had been on drugs during much of that vacation, and an acquaintance characterized her as "somebody hooked on speed." Her tenement landlord said she had moved into her room with "two hippie guys" and that "she had lots of other men up there all the time."

For most families, of course, the situation is quite different. Surveys in the late 1960s disclosed that two of every three young people and seven of every ten parents believed that the generation gap had been exaggerated. Other research shows that youngsters think better of their parents than they ordinarily let on. Daniel Offer and his colleagues found in their Chicago study that a majority of the boys interviewed, while critical of their mothers and fathers, nevertheless considered them not too different from what the boys described as ideal parents. Offer did find that his subjects felt differently about each parent at different times. At about the age of 14, the boys admired their fathers but felt closer to their mothers. Several years later, they were feeling closer to their fathers and better understood by them. When sociologist Frank Musgrove asked 354 English teenagers to complete sentences beginning "Mothers are. . ." "Fathers are. . ." "Mothers can. . ." and "Fathers can. . ." more than two thirds of his subjects had something favorable to say. The results of another study, by psychologist Robert Hess, may surprise adults even more. Hess asked Chicago teenagers to rate their parents on 20 traits such as patience and lovingness, and then he had the parents rate themselves on the same characteristics. On every trait, the children gave their mothers and fathers a higher score than the parents gave themselves.

While the adolescent is struggling to master his sexual impulses and achieve autonomy, he also has to work on the third great problem of his development—deciding what he believes in or, as Erikson expresses it, what to be faithful to. The chief characteristics of this search for values are a cynicism that eventually leads to realism, and an ethical sense that is growing increasingly subtler. According to sociologist Mervyn Cadwallader, the young person is certain that "government is corrupt, the military dehumanizing, the corporations rapacious, the churches organized hypocrisy, and the schools dishonest." Sometimes, Kenneth

continued on page 55

Clutching a stuffed animal for security, a 14-year-old newcomer momentarily reverts to childhood when rebuffed during a tentative attempt to break into the tight world of the Cambridge peer group.

The power of the peers

So important to adolescent development is the peer group—that exclusive band united by age and interests—that one psychiatrist, Irene Josselyn, has said: "Any adolescent who does not conform to some peer group should be observed carefully, since such behavior is so atypical it may suggest incipient serious emotional or mental disturbance." (But not always: there are exceptions, Josselyn hastens to add, who mature better by themselves.)

For most adolescents, the peer group is indispensable because it provides support during a period of rapid physical and emotional changes. Understanding by families counts less as the youngster shakes off dependence; to find his individual identity, he partially rejects his parents and their values.

As a teenager transfers his need for emotional support to his peers, he may submerge his own personality within the group. Like the adolescents in Cambridge, Massachusetts, who are the subject of this picture essay, most peer-group members copy styles, share opinions, communicate in a private language and try out new roles on one another. They spend virtually all their free time together—if not physically, then connected by telephone.

As the Cambridge peers gather on a street corner for a bull session, 15-year-old Thelma stands slightly beyond the circle of friends. A newcomer, she has not been admitted and so she listens to their style of banter and private jokes. As she learns the clique's argot, she will begin taking part and slowly become accepted as a full-fledged, conforming member.

Intimate dancing and nuzzling enjoyed within the security of the group are the Cambridge teenagers' first steps toward sexual contact. After such parties, the youths separate and go home, and seldom pair off except when participating in the joint activities of the clique.

Good-natured clowning by George is
intended to entertain and impress a girl,
Nancy. Because they are members of
the clique, she is unlikely to reproach him
or withdraw from him for showing off.
In this way, the young man can test male
courting behavior, knowing that the
group's sense of loyalty will protect him
from feelings of failure or rejection.

Half-secretive telephone conversations keep Stephanie a part of her peer group even while she is at home. Such constant communication helps the group support members in their drive for autonomy—and strengthens the personal ties that give the group its power.

Keniston found, the young cynic becomes desperately alienated and pessimistic, convinced that there is nothing at all for him to believe in. As one of the youths who was interviewed by Keniston expressed it, "The universe seems dead."

Such research contradicts the assumption that the average adolescent is a romantic, unselfish idealist who cares deeply about humanity and believes that utopia can actually be achieved. When Offer asked his young subjects what they would do with a million dollars, the vast majority said they would save or invest it for their own future or would buy things for themselves. Psychologist Joseph Adelson wrote of "the myth of adolescent idealism." Talking to 450 young Americans, Britons and Germans, Adelson and his colleagues found them at best cautious about the chances of creating an ideal society. Typically, they told him, "You can't change human nature," "There will always be crime" and "People will always disagree."

More noticeable, if less numerous, are the adolescents who are not only optimistic enough to think that the world can be made better but try hard to make it so. Yet even these young activists, Keniston discovered, are not so radical as society thinks. More often than not, they believe in the values their parents preach but perhaps do not practice. Keniston's observations were based on interviews with the leaders of Vietnam Summer, a project created in 1967 by American college students attempting to organize new groups to oppose the war in Southeast Asia. Each student spoke openly about the work he was involved in, his adolescent experiences with family and peers, his feelings about social and political values. All, Keniston found, differed in varying degrees with their families' political views. As one student stated it, "The old structures and institutions of the past no longer fit our needs; therefore we must rebuild." By and large, they accepted the same personal values that their parents upheld—honesty, basic concern for other people, seriousness and responsibility—but were more committed to actively implementing such principles into the fabric of society. One young woman felt that though her parents did not fully understand the depth of her commitment to the Vietnam project—"They knew I was doing something, and they didn't feel too good about it"—they nonetheless supported her decision to take an active part. "At odd times," she remarked, "I can sense that my mother is maybe kind of proud that I'm doing these things."

Most of Keniston's subjects rejected conventional middle-class life. "One thing that took me a long time to learn is that there are models of marriage and adult life but that they don't work. . . . I don't think I

want to live like that," was the way one young person expressed it. Yet the youngsters were not so much alienated as realistic. Such a clear view of life stems from a developing moral sense. The most important research on this topic has been done by psychologist Lawrence Kohlberg. In a series of studies he made in Mexico, in Taiwan and in the United States, Kohlberg posed imaginary moral dilemmas for children and adolescents of all ages. One example: A man's wife will die unless she is treated with a certain drug, but the husband has no money to buy it. Is it right for him to steal it?

Classifying the answers he got, Kohlberg found that they fitted into six levels of moral development, which Kohlberg arbitrarily classified in rising order of desirability. At the lowest level, fear of punishment dictates moral behavior; a child may say that it would not be right for the husband to steal because he might be jailed. At level two, the criterion is selfish need; one child said the man should help himself to the drug because if his wife died, "there will be no one to cook his food." The opinion of others is what counts at level three; theft is wrong because it will bring the perpetrator into disrepute. Level four is the simplistic law-and-order stage; the idea is that all laws, just and unjust alike, must be obeyed no matter what the circumstances. At level five, Kohlberg's subjects became concerned with human rights and suggested that unjust laws ought to be changed. At level six, moral ideas were based on abstract principles of justice (the Golden Rule) and on universal values such as the sanctity of human life. One 16-year-old who had reached this stage told Kohlberg he believed in stealing an essential drug because "human life is above financial gain."

Kohlberg and other researchers who have used his method find that not all adolescents reach the highest ethical levels and that changes occur at different periods of development. Kohlberg found that 20 per cent of the subjects had reached level five at about the age of 18. But two years later they appeared to retrogress to level two, selfish need, only to return to level five by the age of 25.

As if juggling the problems of sexuality, autonomy and values were not enough, the adolescent must also decide what role he is going to play in life. Young people try on roles like clothing. A girl of 13 may appear at breakfast one day as a *femme fatale*, the next as an unkempt hippie. She seems hardly aware that she is acting and becomes indignant if her mother fails to recognize the new self and asks, "Who are you being today?" Frequently a teenager adopts an ornate new handwriting style that seems to fit his new role better than the old one. Sometimes, as if to cement a new identity by an act of near-magic, a youngster picks out a

Embarked on a prolonged hitchhiking trip, two girls walking along a sunny highway in Saskatchewan, Canada, have postponed the decisions that they must eventually make about careers and families. Such a period of delay, which psychoanalyst Erik Erikson calls the psychosocial moratorium, gives young people a time to consider various options before making final adult commitments. The moratorium may include travel, military service, perhaps a temporary job.

new name or insists on spelling the old one in a new way. For example, President Lyndon Johnson's daughter Lucy decided to become Luci when she was 16 years old.

Deep down, the boy or girl at this stage knows that the game of shifting roles is not for keeps. In later adolescence, however, both sexes, but boys especially, begin worrying in earnest about how to earn a living. Erikson believes that "inability to settle on an occupational identity" is what worries adolescents most and Offer's research confirms this conclusion. The biggest single problem of the teen-age boys he studied was deciding on a career.

For all its problems, adolescence is more than a time of turmoil and anguish. It is also a fun-filled time. Offer and his colleagues found in their Chicago study that 18- and 19-year-olds looked back on the years just past with nostalgia. Indeed, many Americans see those years in a rosy glow: hanging out in noisy groups, driving around town in a sports car filled with high-spirited youngsters, cheering at football games, invading the movies in packs or cooking hamburgers at late-night beach parties. Often it is the night of a school dance that really stands out in memory. Even though the "prom" is outmoded in some sophisticated urban centers, it is still a high point of school life in most of the United States. In Cheshire, Connecticut, during the 1970s, a fireman worked extra hours to earn $500, the cost of formal gowns, new shoes and gloves, and elaborate hairdos for his three prom-going daughters. "It's worth it," he said. "It's a night they'll never forget. Put them in high-heel shoes and it's like they're a princess. It makes them feel special, you know?" Cheshire boys felt just as special. Tuxedos were rented, corsages purchased, and combs run through tangled and hitherto unexplored masses of hair. "It's the most important night of the year," the prom chairman said. "You want it to go on forever."

Adolescence is punctuated with memorable experiences, and not the least is the opportunity it often provides for a final burst of childhood freedom—time out from school or other activities in which the young person can find his bearings. Erik Erikson calls this important interval the "psychosocial moratorium," and explains it as a "period of delay granted to somebody who is not ready to meet an obligation."

As an example Erikson cites the case of a girl he calls Jill. An excessively demanding and dependent youngster who was bitterly rivalrous toward the opposite sex, Jill spent a summer on a ranch during her late teens and then rebelled against the idea of going back to college. When she asked to stay on the ranch, her parents granted permission. All at once she stopped demanding to be indulged by oth-

Exuberant, idealistic young Canadians, 2,700 strong, assemble on a bridge linking Windsor, Ontario, and Detroit to protest United States plans to test a nuclear device in the Aleutian Islands. Contrary to popular opinion, adolescents are rarely wild-eyed radicals. More often than not, they subscribe to their parents' values. In this case they were concerned about the environmental effect of the explosion. The tests were carried out nonetheless.

ers. She worked hard looking after newborn colts, getting up in the night to bottle-feed those that needed special attention. When she finally chose to return to college, she was more mature. "She turned 'maternal,'" Erikson said, "but it was a maternalism such as cowboys must and do display; and, of course, she did it all in jeans. This brought recognition 'from man to man' as well as from man to woman, and beyond that the confirmation of her optimism, that is, her feeling that something could be done that felt like her, was useful and worthwhile."

The turmoil and the agony of adolescence is a relatively recent development even in modern, affluent nations, where culture clamps down on the adolescent's sexual urges, restrains his energies, stifles his clamor to grow up and enforces dependency on adults. In the past this stage of life was not nearly so stormy. In many societies today adolescence still proceeds without much turmoil at all.

At one time in Western history, adolescence hardly existed as a distinct period. Childhood ran straight into adulthood, with no waiting period for the child to grow up physically and psychologically. During the Early Middle Ages, boys and girls began to do adult work when they were only five, or at best a year or two older, because there was little time for childhood and none for adolescence. Life was short, and everyone's labor was needed if society was to survive. As existence became less precarious, some people began to advocate the postponement of adulthood. "Leave childhood to ripen in your children," Jean Jacques Rousseau advised in 1762. He also spoke of puberty as a birth into adulthood: "We are born, so to speak, twice over; born into existence, and born into life; born a human being, and born a man." Only three years after Rousseau wrote those words, James Watt invented the steam engine. Thus began the age of the urban technological society with its need for a well-educated and sophisticated populace.

Since the 18th Century adolescence has gradually grown longer. One reason is the increasing complexity of modern society: more and more roles have opened up to young people, making choice more difficult, and because the roles have become more complicated, more time is required to master them. A second reason is that affluence has made it feasible to prolong adolescence; society can now get along without the labor of the young. Yet another element is the fact that physical maturation tends to occur earlier in each succeeding generation, thus stretching out the interval between puberty and full adulthood. A final factor is the development of a special youth culture so attractive to adolescents that they often hate to relinquish it.

But adolescence is not equally long in all parts of modern society. In rural areas, it tends to be shorter than in cities. One study makes this point by quoting from a 1969 account of life on a farming village in East Anglia, England: "The children are very involved with their parents' work and with adult gossip. Quite little boys will know the technical names of tractor attachments and what is going on in the fields at a particular time of the year, and the girls talk together like grown women. Neither seem to want their childhood." In this community and others like it, children are well prepared for adulthood by the time puberty comes, and when it does, few obstacles to adult status are placed in their way. Adolescence is also likely to be fairly short among disadvantaged children in both country and city. Poorer boys and girls have fewer decisions to make because fewer alternatives are available to them, and their roles in life do not generally take so long to learn. Besides, these youngsters need to begin earning a living sooner, and their parents are quicker to grant them sexual and other adult privileges than are upper-class mothers and fathers.

In older cultures, ones that have not yet come into the modern world, the transition from childhood to adulthood may be effected with ease.

In most of these societies puberty is a green light, signaling to the new adolescent that he can move quickly ahead into adulthood. He may have to prove himself as an adult, but he rarely has much to rebel against or to agonize over. He has no bewildering choices to make. There is only one kind of life to live, one religion to follow, one morality to observe. When it comes to sex, that morality is often liberal, permitting guilt-free sexual expression from an early age and thus eliminating a major source of frustration and psychological disturbance. As the Group for the Advancement of Psychiatry points out, there is not much of an identity problem "in simpler societies that offer only two sex-defined role models," the male and the female.

Samoa as described by Margaret Mead was the archetype of tranquil adolescence, the classic example cited by experts as proof that the biological upheaval of puberty does not cause emotional upheaval unless society itself promotes stress. Samoan girls, Mead reported, "were perplexed by no conflicts, troubled by no philosophical queries, beset by

no remote ambitions. To live as a girl with many lovers as long as possible and then to marry in one's own village, near one's own relatives and to have many children, these were uniform and satisfying ambitions." What made growing up so easy for Samoans, the Group for the Advancement of Psychiatry believes, was that Samoan culture allowed adolescents so much sexual freedom. The fact that older brothers and sisters did much of the work of socializing, or bringing up, the young ones also helped. The result: "There is no great disparity in age and power between the socializer and socialized, and this may help explain why Samoans have less anguish over power struggles than do Americans, in whose childhood the parents, comparatively, are omnipresent and seemingly omnipotent."

Samoa is not the only place where adolescence has been simpler than in the West because the local culture made it so. Between the ages of seven and 12, the Shavante boy of Central Brazil goes to live in a bachelors' hut with other boys of his age-set, donning a penis sheath as a symbol of sexual maturity and a sign that childhood is over. He is free to come and go in his village, and he stays in touch with his family. Nevertheless, the fact that he does not live with his parents removes one source of conflict. For five years, the boy builds a sense of solidarity with his fellows and learns the skills of his culture: how to hunt, to make weapons and to plait sleeping mats. He also studies the songs and dances of his people and fashions bead necklaces and other regalia for the ceremonies that will make him an adult. According to anthropologist Lewis Maybury, Shavante bachelors "live a life of carefree ease." They have more leisure than other Shavante, and so much fun that younger boys hang around them in the hope—often realized—of sharing in songs and dances and tagging along on hunting and other group excursions. This adolescent idyll ends when all of the age-set marry simultaneously and take part in initiation rites calling for nothing more arduous than leaping up and down in icy water, making ceremonial runs and participating in dances and feasts.

Such formal rites of passage do much to smooth the way into the grown-up world. Once they are over, everyone recognizes the initiate as an adult. Ordinarily, the rite is scheduled shortly after puberty, leaving little time for development of the kind of turmoil so familiar to the modern world. There is no question about rights and responsibilities. The boy is a man, the girl a woman, with all the duties and privileges accorded those states. With no unsettled questions and few unresolved choices, the turbulence and the agony of adolescence are largely eliminated. But so are the fun-filled, carefree years.

A ritual haircutting initiates young boys into adolescent status among the Shavante of Central Brazil. For the next five years, while they are taught hunting and religious lore, the boys will live together in a bachelor hut at one end of the village and seldom see their families—a semi-isolation that reduces adolescent turbulence by eliminating conflicts with parents and with the society at large.

The Years of Choice

To many it is "the best years of our lives." To others it is a time of stress and painful struggle. For most it is both. This paradox of attitudes toward the attainment of adult status is not so strange as it may seem at first. Beginning at about the age of 20 and continuing throughout the thirties, people find themselves in a new world. They are free. Parents no longer rule them. Society accepts them as full-fledged members and, in turn, offers them the chance to make their contributions to society. They are at the peak of their physical and mental powers —stronger, more handsome, quicker and more alert than they will ever be. The world lies before them, waiting to be grasped.

But precisely because their opportunities are so great, young adults face an equally great responsibility: they must set the patterns for their lives. These years are the years of choice. Decisions must be made, and they are crucial ones. Each young adult must decide finally what work to do, consolidating the choice originally made in adolescence or making a new one if the first no longer seems right. He must make up his mind whether to marry, and when, and whom. Then he must consider whether he wants to become a parent, and if so, when. Once his three choices are made, he must come to terms with them: make a place for himself in the power structure that governs his chosen work; learn to live by himself or, if he marries, with another person under the same roof; adjust to childlessness or to parenthood, to sharing days and nights with a squalling invader.

These tasks may be more difficult for women—particularly if their family responsibilities affect their career opportunities *(left)*—but they cannot be escaped by either sex; whether they are approached directly or stumbled through, they fix the quality of life. But their nature has been viewed in several different ways by the experts. Erik Erikson emphasized the psychological. Young adulthood, he suggested, calls for a crucial inner choice between intimacy and isolation. What Erikson had in mind, he explained, are "intimate relationships, such as friendship, love, sexual intimacy, even intimacy with oneself, one's inner resources, the range of one's excitements and commitments." Courage is required to make intimate commitments, along with the ethical strength to abide by them "even though they may call for significant sacrifices and compromises." Without intimacy, marriage and all other potentially significant ties become meaningless. The result is isolation—a sense of being completely cut off and alone, with no one either to share with or to care for.

Psychologist Daniel Levinson stressed the practical as well as the emotional tasks of young adulthood. At this stage, he believed, the person's goal is to establish a life structure tied to a specific career and a specific person. The young adult begins by exploring possibilities and making tentative commitments to work and to marriage; he ends by putting down roots and creating a definite pattern of life that is ordered, stable, secure and pretty much under his own control. Levinson warned that no one has endless time to achieve these goals. "If a man does not reach a significant start toward settling down by about age 34," Levinson said, "his chances of forming a reasonably satisfying life structure are quite small."

Men and women come to their difficult years of choice lacking in experience and emotional maturity but impressively endowed with other resources for the tasks ahead. Their physical and mental prowess are greater than they have ever been before or will ever be again. Young men are stronger than adolescents. They can work at new jobs with more energy and enthusiasm and for longer periods of time. Women are at the optimum age for motherhood; they are more fully developed and better nourished than teenagers, and they are more likely to give birth to healthy babies; moreover, they have maximum stamina, necessary for taking care of infants.

Both men and women are close to the peak of their intellectual abilities during the years from 18 to 30. Summing up investigations by British and American researchers, the chief psychologist to the Royal Air Force, John Parry, wrote that young adults "assimilate information, make comparisons and deductions and learn new skills more quickly and surely than at any other time in their lives."

How young adults use these peak powers depends on who they are and where they live. The twenties and thirties are years of choice for everyone, but the choices are not necessarily the same. They may be limited or circumscribed by social status, race, economics, custom or the simple facts of geography.

Freedom of occupational choice is chiefly a Western and especially

Concerns of young adults

People do not worry much about their health through their twenties and early thirties *(shaded areas below)*, but their concern rises as they near the end of young adulthood, psychiatrist Roger Gould found in his study of attitude changes through the life cycle *(pages 41 and 103)*. On the other hand, insecurity about marital relationships and about income peaks during this period of family formation.

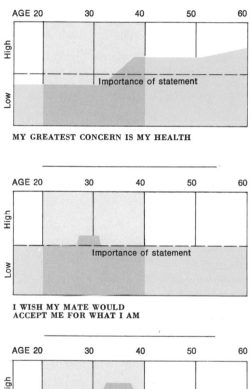

MY GREATEST CONCERN IS MY HEALTH

I WISH MY MATE WOULD
ACCEPT ME FOR WHAT I AM

I DON'T MAKE ENOUGH MONEY TO DO WHAT I WANT

an American phenomenon. For instance, herding is vital to survival among the Aymara Indians of Bolivia, and so every Aymara child is obliged to learn that skill. He begins with pigs when he is only four or five and at 10 reaches the upper limits of his métier: taking charge of more valuable animals like donkeys and cows. Two occupations, herding and hoeing, support the Nyakyusa of Africa, but youngsters cannot decide between them. Beginning at the age of six, they must look after cattle on the grasslands; at 12 they are told to switch to hoeing, the work they pursue for the rest of their lives. But in more developed nations as well, young people often have to take whatever jobs are available without enjoying the luxury of choice. A young woman on a farm in the Scottish Highlands who dreams of producing television shows has little chance of realizing her ambition unless she can make her way to a communications center like London. Poor youths rarely can afford to spend years of training to become physicians, and until recently skin color barred nearly all blacks from elite occupations. Yet these qualifications only underline one of the most remarkable trends of modern life: young people no longer need follow their parents' footsteps. The choice of career is wide, and it poses difficult decisions.

Ordinarily in modern industrial societies young adults are confronted with a task that Levinson called forming an occupation. He found that "initial occupational preferences, even when they seem to be definite choices, usually turn out to be a preliminary definition of interests and values—in science, mechanics, writing, helping people." Most people, he said, do not firmly commit themselves to one occupation even by the early twenties, and many who do later regret their early choice and wish they had investigated the external opportunities more carefully and examined their internal needs more deeply before arriving at a final decision.

The young adult's exploration of inner and outer possibilities is usually illuminated by what Levinson calls "the dream," an aspirational vision of the work he would like to do and the career identity he would like to fashion for himself. The dream "may take a dramatic form," Levinson wrote, "as in the myth of the hero—the great artist, business tycoon, athletic or intellectual superstar performing magnificent feats and receiving unique honors. Developmentally, the crucial question for the young person is how to give the Dream greater shape, to find ways of living it out."

The higher the socioeconomic class, the more ambitious such a dream is likely to be. Economist Eli Ginzberg interviewed young sons of men whose occupations ranged from truck driver to sailor, and he found their dreams were generally modest and practical. They dreamed of achieving an economic level their fathers had not attained. They wanted higher incomes, but in work that was relatively safe and steady. They hoped to learn a skilled trade to give them a leg up the ladder toward the status of a boss. "It is a relatively short step," Ginzberg explains in his book *Occupational Choice*, "for a highly skilled mechanic who has saved part of his earnings to become owner of a garage." Yet Ginzberg found that for most of his subjects, running a business of some kind was "the outer limit of their expectations. No one fantasied about becoming a millionaire, but almost everyone was able to anticipate the possibility of owning a business."

At every level of society, multiple influences direct an individual into his life work. One factor is happenstance. Bronislaw Malinowski used to tell how he had switched from philosophy to anthropology only because he chanced to contract tuberculosis and happened on James Frazer's classic anthropological study *The Golden Bough* while he was convalescing. James McNeill Whistler attributed his artistic career to the fact that he had failed a chemistry examination at the United States Military Academy because he erroneously described silicon as a gas. Years later, he liked to insist to his friends, "Had silicon been a gas, I would have been a major general."

The effect of chance is not quite what it seems, Ginzberg pointed out. Almost everyone's life is filled with random events that theoretically could trigger important consequences but usually pass unnoticed. They have little effect because the young adult, still in the process of forming an occupation, pays attention only to those chance happenings that strike a responsive chord in his soul; career choices are influenced less by random external events than by the individual's social and economic background and inner emotional needs, both conscious and unconscious.

Children with exceptional gifts—in music or art or mathematics—rarely have difficult career decisions to make because an intense urge to express their special abilities nearly always dominates their lives. Young adults who suffered painful traumas in childhood sometimes try to come to terms with them in their work. Psychoanalyst Theodore Lidz reported that he "once studied three prizefighters and could not fail to note that all three had brutal fathers whom they had vowed to beat up when they were old enough and strong enough."

A much more common influence on career choice is a need to stand high in the eyes of the world. Goaded by this very human desire, the young adult weighing a possible career considers not only the pleasure but also the prestige it is likely to bring him. According to psychologist

Rosalind Barnett, "there is almost universal agreement about the relative prestige of a large number of occupations," with both children and adults ranking them in about the same order. In the 1970s medicine headed nearly all lists of preferred careers in the United States and had done so for years. In 1950 a Gallup poll found that 29 per cent of Americans questioned thought it the best profession; in 1973 the figure was 28 per cent. On the whole, prestige occupations do not fluctuate greatly from generation to generation. However, Gallup found that law gained a little prestige between 1950 and 1973: in the earlier year, 8 per cent of Americans had ranked it first, compared to 14 per cent in 1973. And when the American Council on Education surveyed 188,900 students in 1972, it found a slackening of interest in engineering and the physical sciences, accompanied by rising interest in the health and other people-oriented professions.

Whatever the influences that shape the occupational dream, it remains little more than a dream for a long time; most of the young adult years are devoted to realizing it. Of the 40 men Levinson studied, about half got substantial psychological help in making it come true from someone Levinson dubs "the mentor." Usually a teacher, boss, colleague or friend who is eight to 15 years older than the young adult, the mentor "takes a younger man under his wing, invites him into a new occupational world, shows him around, imparts his wisdom, cares, sponsors, criticizes and bestows his blessing. . . . He fosters the young adult's development by believing in him, by sharing the Dream." This elder guide is not a phenomenon unique to Levinson's small group. In the 1970s, Harvard psychiatrist George Vaillant, following up on a study of 250 Harvard men that had begun in 1938, found that 90 per cent of the men (who were by then in late middle age) had had an adviser fitting Levinson's description while those who had not, or who had not found one until they were in their forties, proved to be rather unsuccessful in their careers.

The intense relationship between an elder associate and young adult lasts from three to 12 years, coming to an end when the younger person reaches his mid-thirties. Occasionally the relationship turns into a friendship between equals. More often the young person decides that the man he had once idealized has feet of clay and comes to see him as "a tyrannical and egocentric father rather than a loving, enabling Mentor." This altered judgment usually has less to do with the individual's real qualities than with the fact that the young adult is outgrowing his need for a guide. To help himself break free of this dependence he be-

A trio of agile Masai warriors prove their physical prowess in the synchronized leaps of a tribal dance called the eranyata. Often performed after a lion hunt, the dance is symbolic of the dependence of the tribe upon the strength and alertness of young men who protect the herds from predators.

comes unfairly critical, behaving exactly as he did when it was time to leave the protection of his parents in adolescence. Levinson points out that this declaration of adult independence occurred twice in dramatic fashion during the career of Sigmund Freud. As a young man, he looked to physician Josef Breuer as his guide, but when he was ready to strike out on his own, he quarreled with Breuer. Later, warmth and admiration similarly turned to bitterness when Freud's own protégé, Carl Jung, rebelled against him in turn.

The elder colleague is not the only special friend who helps the young adult establish himself. Levinson found that his male subjects focused on a female figure, "the Special (loved and loving) Woman." She may be girl friend or wife—but need not be. Like the mentor, she helps a man in pursuit of his goals. "She enables him to sustain the Dream by sharing in it, by believing in him as its hero, by joining him on the journey," Levinson said, adding that she creates a climate "in which aspirations can be imagined and hopes nourished." Similarly, Levin-

As if propelled by springs, limber-legged British athletes bounce upward for a ball during a soccer match between Arsenal and Manchester United. Such fast-paced contests enable young males to display their stamina and fitness before appreciative, emotionally charged crowds.

son found from interviews with the wives of his male subjects that as women's expectations and opportunities have enlarged in recent years they have looked more and more to their husbands for support in fulfilling their dreams.

A partner in marriage is the second great choice of the young adult. It is a dual choice. While every person must find some kind of life work, not everyone gets married. Thus the first part of this choice is between a married life and a single one. If the decision is for marriage, that still leaves the question, to whom?

Ordinarily marriage is a *sine qua non* of growing up, but even in tradition-bound countries the custom may be less rigid than is often thought. In 1975 the governing council of the Nkonya district in Ghana, West Africa, saw fit to issue an edict calling on all girls to get married within six months or pay a fine of $12, one live sheep and a pot of palm wine (the idea was to stamp out prostitution). But there was no guarantee the edict would be obeyed. Pauline Adansi of the Ghanaian

Women's Society for Public Affairs was frankly skeptical. "Suppose a girl is not interested in getting married and pays a fine. What next? The Nkonya Council could end up with almost as many sheep as there are girls in the neighborhood."

In the West, no law requires either men or women to marry, but social pressure to do so is considerable, and its effects are detectable even on the very young. A 1968 study of 1,639 young people from 10 to 12 years old by Carlfred Broderick and George Rowe found that 84 per cent of the girls and 62 per cent of the boys already took their own eventual marriage for granted. Nearly three fourths of the youngsters already had a girl or boyfriend, and of this group 66 per cent claimed to have been in love at least once.

In the years after 1968, staying single became an increasingly acceptable alternative to marriage. However, reports about the carefree life of the "swinging singles" are greatly exaggerated. "Society is sort of geared like Noah's Ark; everything is supposed to be in pairs after the age of 35," said Lynn Shelton. An airline stewardess aged 47 who had never been married, Miss Shelton led a discussion entitled "How to be Happy, Though Single" for 65 men and women members of City Singles, a Manhattan-based club for the unmarried. Raising their hands in answer to a question, nearly all of the group said that they were happy —but all except two indicated that they would like to get married. "Loneliness is the looming threat of the single life. There is no way of beating it," commented Harvard sociologist Robert Weiss. Weiss noted that a married person may be miserable, but at least he has built-in companionship. The single person, however, must spend much of his time and energy looking for companionship. "The great thing about marriage," Weiss thinks, "is that it gives you time to do other things. If you're not married, your life is a lot of bounce from one relationship to another: finding somebody, nurturing the relationship, losing it, then finding somebody else."

Finding someone to marry, if that is what the young adult wants to do, is simpler in some cultures than in others. Often the young person has little say in the matter; arranged marriages are still common in some parts of the world. The negotiators, usually the parents, are generally more concerned with protecting the social and economic interests of their respective families than with promoting their children's marital happiness. In rural Greece, for example, a father traditionally makes his children a present of land when they marry, but he tries to keep control of it in family hands by choosing distant cousins as marital partners for his offspring. In some small Egyptian villages, marriages between first cousins are preferred. The parents' assumption is that the mates will be especially cooperative with each other because of the closeness of their family ties.

Even in modern societies, old patterns often determine who marries whom. In Japan, matchmakers engaged by parents were still arranging more than a third of all marriages during the early 1970s. But postwar Japan has seen the development of a more impersonal matchmaker, the marriage bureau. Run sometimes by private operators, sometimes by government agencies, the new bureaus ask applicants about their income, health and attitudes before arranging a *miai* (literally, seeing each other) between two possibly congenial young people. The giant Mitsubishi company set up a marriage service of its own in 1973, using a computer to match employees who wanted to find mates and were willing to pay a $30 fee for promising leads. Eight courtship counselors, nearly all of them wives of company executives, helped workers make final choices. Mitsubishi's purpose was pragmatic. The service cut down the time and money employees would otherwise spend finding a partner. And it helped make employees better workers. Said an executive, "When the wife shares the same corporate frame of reference with her husband, she can only understand him more and help achieve for him a higher degree of performance and efficiency."

Marriage bureaus are also flourishing in Germany, where war and economic progress have disrupted traditional meeting patterns. Between 1945 and 1975, some 240 marriage agencies sprang up. Although many were operated by swindlers or incompetents, one agency, the largest of its kind in the world, proved not only reputable but proficient. Like Mitsubishi, the Altmann Institute in Hamburg relies on a giant computer, but it also has a staff of 250 technicians, psychological researchers and marriage counselors. In contrast to the average American dating service, which asks applicants for only the skimpiest data about themselves, the institute gathers extensive information about every client's personal and psychological characteristics before searching out a suitable partner. Close to 200,000 men and women of all ages consult Altmann every year, of whom 50 per cent are rejected as unlikely prospects. At any one time, there is a roster of about 30,000 marriage candidates in the files. Each pays a fee of approximately $1,300 and gets as many as 300 names to choose from over a three-year period. About 5,000 marriages are arranged every year. (A study of Altmann's results over a period of 10 years by anthropology professor Hans Jürgen of Kiel University showed that the computer-arranged alliances were nearly three times

Each hoping that his physical beauty will win the approval of a young maiden, Bororo men bedecked in beads and cowrie shells dance before old men and women in the first stage of a courtship ceremony that leaves final choice to the girls.

Friends help a Bororo youth prepare for the festival dance, the gerewol, in which the unmarried women among these nomadic herders will choose a mate. The men here are adjusting a cotton headband pulled back to accentuate the youth's high forehead—a highly prized feature.

Pondering the choice of a husband, Bororo maidens kneel and consider the merits of each of the dancers judged eligible for marriage.

Male beauty contest to pick a husband

At the annual festival marking the end of the rainy season, the nomadic Bororo of West Africa permit the women of their tribe to select their mates. For young Bororo males, this reversal of the usual mate-selecting process can be an ego-bruising experience.

The Bororo gather together every September for feasting, cattle trading and—most important—marriage settlements. The marriage transactions focus upon dances that permit the young men to exhibit their physical beauty.

Dressed in their finery, the young men form a line and begin singing and rhythmically stamping their feet. During this dance, called the *yakey*, old men and women appraise the youths and brutally insult those who are considered ugly. These unfortunates retire, and the more acceptable men participate in a second dance, the *gerewol*, before eligible young women. At the end of this courtship dance, the women select their favorites—first as lovers, and subsequently as husbands.

more successful than marriages that came about by accidental meeting of the marital partners.)

Most people in contemporary societies choose their husbands and wives without assistance from marriage bureaus or computers. Behavioral scientists have formulated many theories about what it is that attracts an individual to a prospective mate, but none of these is subject to proof. The likelihood is that no one theory will explain everyone's marital choice, and that almost any reasonable hypothesis will have some validity for someone.

Carl Jung believed that every human being is born with an archetype of the perfect mate, an internal idealized image of the person he wants to marry that is colored and shaped after birth by the individual's experience and by the way he perceives his parents as a child. When an adult finds someone in real life who seems to match this idealized figure, he often decides to get married, even though he may subsequently learn that his view of the right helpmeet was illusory. Freud thought that a person tends to marry someone like his opposite-sexed parent, to make up for the disappointment he felt as a child when he realized he could never marry his parent. As a matter of fact, patients in psychoanalysis often—but by no means always—discover that this was exactly what influenced their choice of a partner.

A study conducted at the University of Toronto by psychologist Arthur Aron found evidence for an intriguingly different explanation. He concluded that both men and women may choose someone like their mothers to marry (although Aron warned that the results are preliminary). Using a dozen of his students as researchers, Aron went to the marriage license bureau in Toronto city hall, handed out questionnaires to everyone standing in line, and asked each man and woman to mark down the answers without comparing notes with his future spouse. The questions were about certain characteristics—trust, responsiveness, playfulness—that each person had noticed in the relationship with parents and that were now seen in the future spouse. Subjects were asked to choose between pairs of alternatives such as "I feel my secrets are safe with my future wife," and "My future wife makes promises she doesn't keep." Similar questions were asked of the future wife and about both parents ("My mother used to make promises she didn't keep"). When the answers were tabulated, Aron found that in a significant number of instances people described their relationships with their mothers and with their partners in the same way; a man who had trusted his mother often trusted his wife-to-be as well, and his wife-to-be was more likely to feel the same way about her mother, not her father. Aron's conclu-

Quarreling into marriage

Many young adults whose choices of mates ultimately prove sound may come to their decision stormily. Their passage to the altar is strewn with quarrels, some loud and bitter. Psychiatrists say that these lovers' quarrels can be useful. They clear the air, relieve tensions and aggressions, and in the long run may lead to better understanding.

In the heat of a quarrel people often say what they really mean, revealing sides of themselves—deep-seated fears, vanities, uncertainties—that otherwise would never come to light. The quarreling couple may thus get to know and appreciate each other more deeply than they would if they did not fight.

sion: "Both men and women seek to repeat in marriage the relationship they had with their mother."

A third widely held view of the mate-selection process holds that human beings marry someone like themselves. Many studies of husbands and wives have shown that marriage partners are quite similar. The trouble with most of these studies is that they tested people after they were married, or at least after they had known each other a long time. This time factor raises the possibility that the partners were unlike each other when they first met and became similar only after they had joined forces. There had seemed to be no way of testing that possibility: how can a researcher know ahead of time who is going to end up marrying whom? Then sociologist Eloise Snyder found an ingenious way around the difficulty by using a group of young people whom she could follow over several years.

Snyder's experiment was conducted in two steps. First she studied the entire population—561 all told—of the sophomore classes in 13 rural schools in Pennsylvania, asking each youngster whether he approved or disapproved of 14 different kinds of behavior ranging from going to church and dancing, to spending money freely and wearing make-up. Then Snyder waited to see whom the students chose to marry. After several years, she found 20 married couples paired off from among her original subjects. When she went back and looked up their attitudes as she had measured them before the couples began dating, she found that as students they had been alike in not much more than half of their personal opinions. These 20 couples, at least, did not seem to have chosen each other for the compatibility of their attitudes before marriage. Snyder did not find it practical to retest the partners to see if they had grown more alike after they were married, but she theorized that they might have done so.

No matter how carefully parents, counselors, computers or couples themselves choose partners for marriage, the decision to marry one person rather than all others is bound to be something of a gamble. Some cultures sanction trial marriage to lower the odds against marital failure. The Peruvian Indians of Vicos in the Andes have been practicing trial marriage for 400 years. The experiment lasts an average of 15 months and leads to actual marriage 83 per cent of the time. In the Pacific, the Trobriand Islanders used to provide a "bachelor's house" where couples could share sex—but not meals or other intimacies—before marriage.

Relatively few cultures institutionalize such experiments, but nearly all sanction some kind of equivalent. One is the engagement period.

The fact that it can help test the wisdom of marital choice is suggested by a 1945 study by sociologists Ernest Burgess and Harvey Locke. Surveying married college graduates, they found that a third of the wives and a fourth of the husbands had been through a broken engagement to someone else before making a final choice. Another substitute for trial marriage is simply living together. Some experts think that even when such arrangements work well (and they often do), there is no assurance that marriage will also succeed. Arlene Skolnick, a sociologist at the University of California, explains why: "Marriage is *not* a continuation of what went before; it is a whole new sort of thing. . . . Before, a couple may have had a feeling of being two separate individuals living together. Now they are two lives meshing together."

Because so many adjustments must be made by a newly wed couple, their first years together are as often marked by stress as by bliss. So serious is the stress that divorce statistics from a dozen key states show that more than half of all marital breakups occur within the first five years. Psychiatrist Robert Ravich, associate director of family therapy at Payne Whitney Clinic in New York, believes that in the early years of marriage, "space and time are the fundamental issues." When they marry, Ravich explained, two people suddenly find themselves in limited space for long periods of time. Each person erroneously assumes that the other is following the same inner timetable, one to which he himself is so accustomed that it seems the only logical schedule for living. The task is to work out mutually acceptable new patterns for bathing, eating, getting ready to go out, having sex and all the other major and minor activities of everyday life.

Ravich wrote of one couple whose spatial and temporal incompatibility was so great that they could not resolve their differences. When first married they lived in a large apartment and got along well, but when they had to move into smaller quarters, they fought constantly in its confines. Eventually they separated. The husband took a job in another city, rented a large house, and persuaded his wife to try again. A second separation came after they moved into yet another small apartment. Finally the couple hit on a solution. They set up house in separate apartments and found that if they could spend more time apart they got on well when they were together.

Few couples can identify for themselves such subtle causes of dissension. When three University of Pennsylvania psychiatrists studied 300 families in an effort to identify the principal causes of marital disagreement, the reasons reported were the familiar ones. Money ranked as the main source of contention, followed by managing the household, sex, sharing housework, disciplining children and spending leisure time. Mothers-in-law also scored high as a source of irritation, the husband's mother outranking the wife's.

A similar list of argument-provokers turned up in a later study when sociologist Irving Tallman of the University of California took a close look at 240 families in Riverside, California, a suburban community not far from Los Angeles. Oddly enough, he did find one source of conflict that did not show up at all in the earlier study: among Riverside husbands and wives, the most incendiary topic was which television and radio programs to turn on.

If underlying difficulties are not too serious, fighting can clear the air, according to psychologist George R. Bach. He maintains, "Couples who fight together stay together." Partners who are afraid to quarrel because they think conflict destroys a marriage are doomed to live in what Bach calls pseudo-intimacy. "A marriage that operates on the after-you-my-dear-Alphonse principle may last a lifetime—a lifetime of fake accommodations, monotony, self-deception and contempt."

The choice of a mate is left to the stars in northern Indian villages such as Dewata, where a Hindu father (left) watches as his daughter's birth date is checked by an astrologer against those of possible husbands. Only a young man whose zodiacal sign is compatible with the girl's will be an acceptable match for her.

Bach believes that only fair fights are therapeutic, and he has evolved a set of rules that he teaches to groups of couples in "fight-training sessions." One rule is "Request a time and place" by saying something like, "Hey, I've got a bone to pick with you." This approach avoids surprise attacks and makes quarrels voluntary. A second rule is "Don't drop the bomb on Luxembourg"—i.e., a mountainous grievance should not be made out of a molehill annoyance. Yet another guideline is "Make sure it's over." Bach's suggestion is to ask, "Have you got it all off your chest?"

Quarreling or not, the great majority of young people enjoy marriage, and they enjoy it more during these youthful years than they will later. Angus Campbell of the Institute for Social Research at the University of Michigan reported that marriage seems to make people happy. Campbell's research team interviewed a rigorously prepared, statistically random sample of 2,164 Americans—a group of a size and composition to make their responses an accurate reflection of the feelings of the entire United States population. The researchers asked their subjects about their overall feelings of satisfaction or dissatisfaction. They also gave each person eight pairs of adjectives, such as interesting/ boring, and asked which best applied to the subject's life. Although the investigators found many married people who were miserable and many singles who were contented, the average husband or wife was far happier and more satisfied with life than the average single person. Of all age groups, young marrieds in their twenties were happiest of all, especially the wives. "They are positively euphoric," Campbell wrote. "They are the most likely group to enjoy doing housework, which single women consider drudgery. It appears that marriage is still considered a woman's greatest achievement, and when she marries, the sigh of relief is almost audible."

Interestingly enough, Campbell and his co-workers found that while single women were less content than married women, they were physically and psychologically healthier. Older single women proved to be less unhappy than younger ones. "Perhaps," Campbell speculated, "this is because the longer a woman remains single, the more she likes it, or at least adjusts to it." A second factor, he suggests, may be that older single women are likely to have better-paying and more satisfying jobs than their younger counterparts. Another finding was that at all ages, single women are more content than single men. "So much for the stereotype of the carefree bachelor and the anxious spinster; the truth is that there are more carefree spinsters and anxious bachelors," Campbell wrote.

Until recently, a normal marriage inevitably and quickly produced children. There was no choice. Today, too, societies generally expect married couples to have children, and few men and women want to defy that tradition. But now the increasing availability of contraceptives has made choices possible for many people. By 1974, the United Nations reported, 115 nations permitted the sale of contraceptives, while contraception was limited or banned completely in 23 nations. Particularly in the wealthier countries, young adults can decide whether or not they want to have a child. In some ways the decision to have children is more crucial than the choice of an occupation or a mate, because it is irreversible. "We can have ex-spouses and ex-jobs but not ex-children," sociologist Alice Rossi noted.

In the United States, voluntary childlessness has become more acceptable than it used to be. Judith Leiber, wife of the Washington, D.C., painter Gerson Leiber, says frankly that she and her husband feel no need of children, and she adds, "I hope my husband will be remembered by his work. Who remembers how many kids Reubens or Rembrandt had?" Her decision, however, remains the minority choice. Government statistics for 1974 indicate that close to 90 per cent of all married American couples had children. The figures were 90 per cent for England, 88 per cent for France, 85 per cent for Germany and 88 per cent for Japan.

The decision to have children brings more than the responsibility of another mouth to feed and the delight of young laughter. Although doctors have long known a great deal about the physical aspects of pregnancy, they have only recently begun to study its psychological consequences. Some of the most interesting observations have come from psychoanalyst Max Deutscher of New York. Over a period of several years, Deutscher has interviewed many couples and studied their dreams and fantasies during and after pregnancy. Most of his subjects were not psychiatric patients but healthy, well-adjusted women (and their husbands) who were admitted to the obstetric clinic at Roosevelt Hospital in New York. Deutscher's chief conclusion: Pregnancy is not a time of passive waiting but "a profound, transforming experience for the young adult." While a baby is being formed physically, Deutscher says, a family is being created psychologically.

Deutscher found that the transformation of marriage partners into parents goes through three stages, each of which lasts about three months. The first trimester is a time of shock during which husband and wife normally begin to recognize that nothing will ever be the same

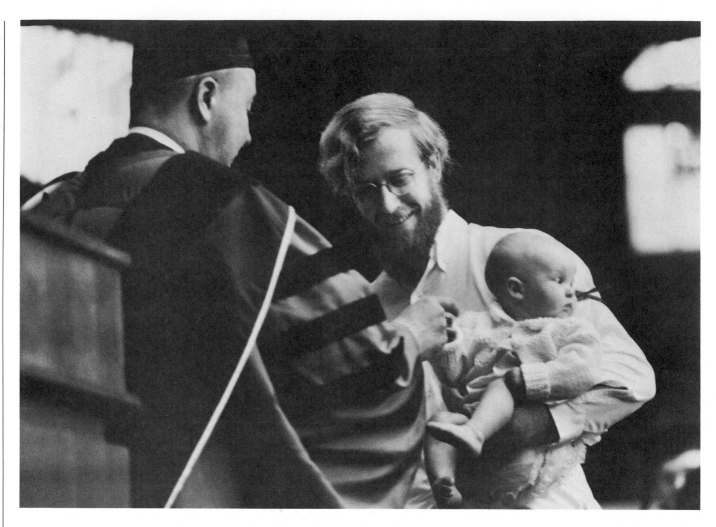

again. If they do not perceive the impending change, they are in for trouble. "People who don't feel that anything is different are not going to create anything different," Deutscher warned. These first three months also provide an opportunity for the couple to practice parenthood. The husband becomes paternal because his wife is now more dependent, both physically and psychologically, and the wife is often maternal toward her husband—he may lean on her out of fear that he will soon lose her to the baby.

The second trimester is more peaceful—and more fun. With the quickening, Deutscher found, couples play with the wife's abdomen, "pushing it to call forth a response from the fetus." Often, he said, there is "a sense of hilarity and awe, of joking and solemnity, and of some quality of respect" that is almost religious. The baby begins to seem human. The mother talks to it ("Let's go shopping today") and if her activities are strenuous, she imagines that the baby experiences the same tiredness she does. Happy couples are now likely to give the un-

Most young people make the big decisions
of early adulthood one at a time.
This smiling young man, graduating from
Amherst College, has lumped three
—opting for a wife, a child and education
for a career during the same time span.

born infant a name; maladjusted ones may simply call it "the monster," or "the thing."

During the final three months before the baby arrives, the couple's increasingly obvious sexual differences help the woman to feel more feminine and the man to enjoy his masculinity more, thus enhancing their emotional relationship. This is also the time when fears of death come to the fore. (Deutscher wrote of one husband who became concerned for his wife after he had watched a film on childbirth. Soon afterward he dreamed of his wife's giving birth painlessly to nine cellophane-wrapped babies in cardboard boxes.)

The birth of a child is almost universally an occasion for rejoicing. The Fang woman of West Africa, after having her baby in her parents' home, carries the infant triumphantly to her husband's house. In modern Japan, the company that employs the husband rewards the arrival of the first child with an increased family allowance. But after mother and baby have come home from the hospital, reality sets in, and it can be painful—even disastrous *(pages 88-99)*. In the 1950s, sociologist E. E. LeMasters of Beloit College interviewed 46 couples who had recently had children; 38 of them—83 per cent—reported "extensive" or "severe" crisis in adjusting to their first child. It was not that the parents had not wanted a baby; 35 of the pregnancies in the "crisis" families had been planned or at least desired.

The cause of the trouble was the same one that triggers so much unhappiness in marriage: poor preparation and false, romantic expectations. "We knew where babies came from," one mother told LeMasters, "but we didn't know what they were like." The wives, LeMasters found, had not known how exhausted they would get, how much they would be confined at home or how much guilt they would feel at not being better mothers. The fathers had not realized that their wives would become sexually less responsive for a while. They had not realized, either, that they themselves would experience money worries and a general, though perhaps temporary, disenchantment with parenthood.

"The patter of little feet aggravates as well as delights," Angus Campbell discovered. "Almost as soon as a couple has kids, their happy bubble bursts. For both men and women, reports of happiness and satisfaction drop to average, not to rise again significantly until their children are grown and about to leave the nest." Parents of older children proved to be among the happiest groups that Campbell studied, leading him to conclude that "raising a family seems to be one of those tasks, like losing weight or waxing the car, that is less fun to be doing than to have done."

The difficult task of adjusting to the three important choices made by the young adult usually leads to a time of stocktaking at the midpoint of early adulthood. Daniel Levinson named this point, which extends from about 28 to 33, the "age 30 transition." Levinson explained that "life is becoming more serious now, more restrictive, more for real," prompting the feeling that "if I want to change my life—if there are things in it that I don't like, or things missing that I would like to have—this is the time to make a start, for soon it will be too late." At this time the young adult decides either to hold the course he had earlier set or to change direction. In either case he comes, after four or five years, to a period of settling down, a time of order, stability, security and control, but also of planning, striving, moving upward, and setting specific goals and dates for reaching them. "The executive has to get into the corporate structure by age 40," Levinson wrote, "the assistant professor has to get tenure by 40, and so on."

Only 20 per cent of the men Levinson studied had a fairly smooth transition to the settling-down period; 60 per cent went through a moderate or severe crisis. One of those who endured a hard time was a black novelist from a lower-middle-class family who was dividing his time between writing and earning enough at a steady job to support his family. Tragically, "he had shaped a Dream of a life alien" to his wife. She did not share his cultural interests, and she could not conceive of writing as a legitimate way of life. At the age of 29, the novelist felt impelled to do one of the most painful things he could imagine: he abandoned his wife and family in order to be able to continue with his writing. "He had to," Levinson says, "his soul was at stake." He went through a dismal period of decline, during which he drifted through a series of jobs. Only when he reached the age of 34 did he finally begin to inch ahead; gradually he came to think of himself as being genuinely a writer and to make writing his primary occupation.

After this settling-down period, the next step for all young adults is a new kind of independence that Levinson describes as "becoming one's own man." If the subject is a writer, he wants to feel unintimidated by his publisher and invulnerable to critical attack. If he is a businessman, he longs for the authority to make his own decisions and "to get the enterprise really going." This ultimate breaking away from the restraints of family and custom marks a new high in assertiveness and confidence. To Levinson it is "a time of peaking and culmination," representing "the high point of early adulthood." The individual who reaches this level is now a fully developed human being; he expects respect for what he is—and he is worthy of it.

A marriage that failed

The feelings of hope and joy, passion and tenderness that surround two of the most important decisions of young adulthood—to marry and to have children—can conceal the true importance of those choices. Years may pass before their full significance is realized.

On the surface, the couple at right appeared idyllically suited to each other when they decided in the summer of 1959 to marry. Will McBride was a dashing young American photographer, Barbara Wilke an intelligent, attractive German girl of 19. They met in Berlin and, Barbara recalls, it was a case of "love at first sight." They shared an interest in poetry and painting. She was attracted to the glamor that surrounded him as an expatriate photographer in Berlin's art colony; Will found in her a quiet shyness that appealed to something deep in him. Within three months they married; shortly after, Barbara became pregnant.

As a professional photographer, Will recorded (or had friends record) their early meetings, their wedding and the birth of their first child. It seemed that he was merely chronicling the story of a happy marriage. But beneath the surface important changes were taking place in the relationship. The young couple who had been attracted to each other in such romantic fashion were growing apart. Two more sons were born, and the McBrides struggled valiantly to hold their marriage together. But then, after 10 years, they finally separated and were later divorced. To both of them, that seemingly innocuous family album now appears in a different light. Looking at the pictures of a happier time, both Will and Barbara find symptoms of the breakup to come.

Holidaying in Germany shortly after they met, Will McBride, a young American photographer, and Barbara Wilke, a German who wanted to be an antique dealer, talked of poetry—and of marriage. "I was thrilled by the intense relationship," Barbara remembers, "We almost instantly decided to marry."

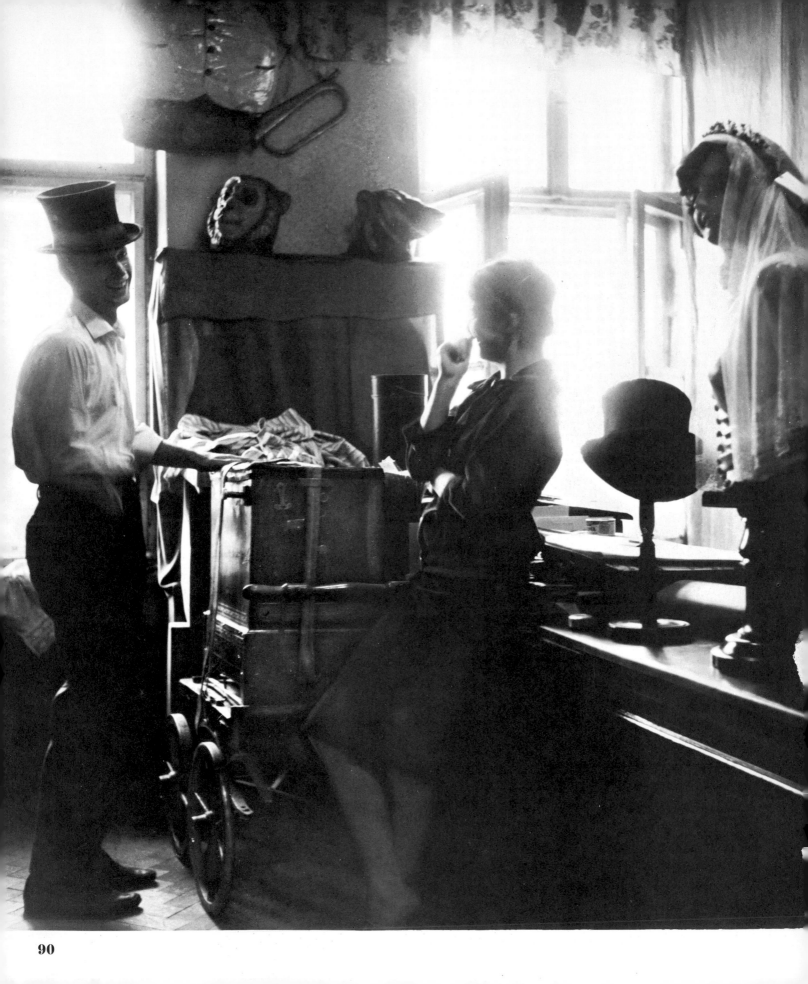

In what could be a scene from a fairy-tale wedding, the golden sun of a September afternoon dapples a country lane taking Will and Barbara to the church where they were married.
The couple resolved one potential conflict soon after the ceremony, when Will decided not to return to America but to stay in Europe to pursue his career.

The betrothed pair share a laugh as Will tries on a top hat in a wedding accessories store in Berlin. "I had the feeling," Will said later, "that when I married Barbara I was marrying all of Europe and two thousand years of tradition."

*Pregnant shortly after her marriage,
Barbara sits wearily by herself at a party,
while Will—reflected in the mirror
—photographs the get-together.
Pregnancy forced Barbara and Will to
limit their active social life; they
felt out of place among their old friends,
most of whom were not married.*

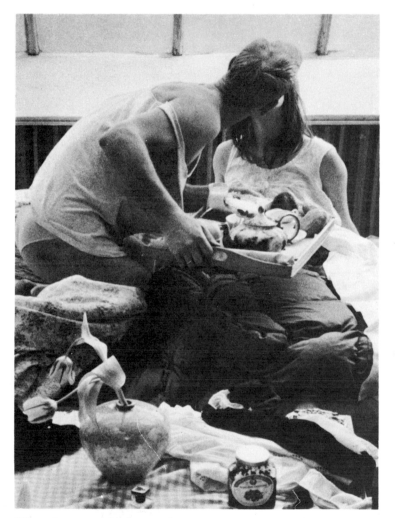

"Now there are only the two of us, you and I," Will wrote lovingly about the months before the baby was born, when he often left the apartment early to buy fresh bread and served breakfast in bed to Barbara. Barbara too, remembers this period of waiting as exciting and beautiful. "There was not a hint of the difficulties to come," she says.

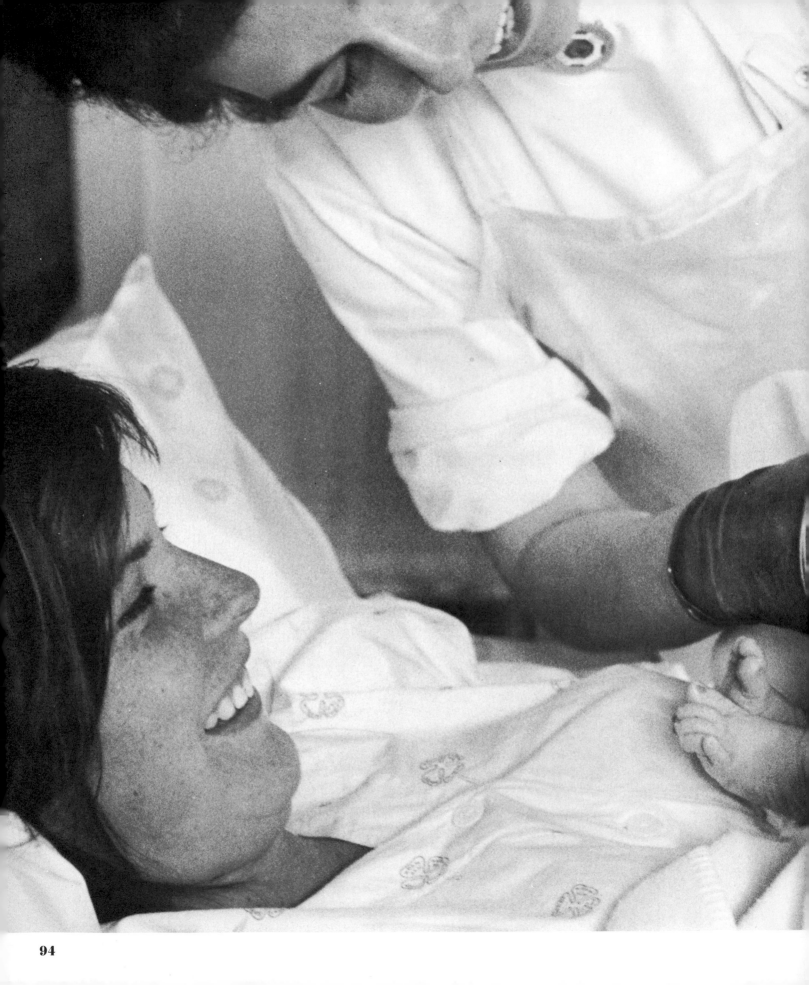

94

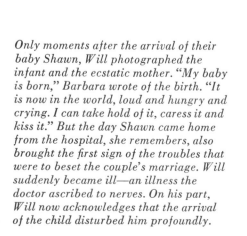

Only moments after the arrival of their baby Shawn, Will photographed the infant and the ecstatic mother. "My baby is born," Barbara wrote of the birth. "It is now in the world, loud and hungry and crying. I can take hold of it, caress it and kiss it." But the day Shawn came home from the hospital, she remembers, also brought the first sign of the troubles that were to beset the couple's marriage. Will suddenly became ill—an illness the doctor ascribed to nerves. On his part, Will now acknowledges that the arrival of the child disturbed him profoundly.

At home, Barbara focuses her time and attention on the infant. Will gave up his studio, which became the nursery, and he felt deprived of her comfort, Barbara says, adding, "I tried to give him as much time as I could spare but it was not enough." Both now see that though they already were beginning to grow apart, they did not recognize it at the time. Will was jealous of their son; Barbara envied Will's freedom to go on assignments while she remained at home with Shawn.

Wiping her brow in apparent tension, Barbara stands by as Will and his associates crowd into the apartment to pore over photographs for an intended book. Shawn, whose room was next to Will's darkroom, "cried when I was in there trying to develop and print my pictures," Will says. As the stresses mounted, Barbara devoted more time to the baby and Will more to his work.

When Will and Barbara McBride sat for this photograph with Shawn, a year after his birth, they appeared—and still felt themselves to be—a loving young family. And yet the baby had irrevocably changed their relationship, and with it their feelings for each other. Years after their divorce, Will said of the baby, "I felt its arrival as a tremendous loss, and have never got over it. I wanted Barbara all to myself." Barbara agrees that she and Will, as a couple, were never able to adjust to the presence of their first child.

Facing Middle Age

4

It may happen suddenly or gradually, but the pattern is always much the same. At the age of 40, perhaps, or at 45 or 50, an individual can see for himself that he has arrived at a halfway house, a midpoint in the adult years *(left)*. More than half of life is gone and, in the words of American writer James Baldwin, "When more time stretches behind than stretches before one, some assessments, however reluctantly and incompletely, begin to be made."

For many, the assessment takes the form of a new perspective upon time itself and upon the possibilities of personal change, a perspective in which experience is seen in terms of "time-left-to-live" rather than "time-since-birth." As one man put it, "It's as if you've gotten to the top of a hill and now you can see all the way down to the other side. You're not going to suddenly fall off, but now you can see to the end." For others, midlife brings new insight and self-understanding, often in unexpected ways. A woman found herself at an intersection of the generations within her own family. "It is as if there are two mirrors before me," she said, "each held at a partial angle. I see part of myself in my mother who is growing old, and part of her in me. In the other mirror I see part of myself in my daughter. I have had some dramatic insights just from looking in those mirrors . . . a set of revelations that I suppose can come only when you are in the middle of three generations."

Such fresh perspectives generally come as the fruit of conscious stock-taking and long reflection. Far more subtle and sometimes only half-conscious are internal signals that herald the beginning of the midlife period. Some of these cues are biological: bodies thicken, skin wrinkles, a contemporary suddenly dies of a heart attack, or a man who feels mentally young notices that his son consistently wins at tennis. But the psychological indications are perhaps more significant. The father who sees his son overtake and pass him physically soon detects a widening gap in shared experiences not only between him and his children but also between him and those who seemed his peers. A middle-aged office worker told Bernice Neugarten, the University of Chicago psychologist who studied aging, that one trivial social difference had been the turning point: "I used to think that all of us in the office were contemporaries, for we all had similar career interests. But one day we were talking about old movies and we realized that the younger ones had never seen a Shirley Temple film. . . . Then it struck me with a blow that I was older than they. I had never been so conscious of it before."

What this man came to realize in a casual office conversation, others arrive at in an astonishing variety of ways—but the ways have certain underlying patterns. Neugarten established a number of these patterns. In a series of studies involving more than 2,000 men and women, for example, she demonstrated that the cues by which the onset of midlife is perceived vary significantly according to sex. Women, she found, take their cues from happenings within the family—moving to a bigger house, the maturing of children and, most important of all, the point at which children marry or leave home. Even unmarried career women, she observed, "often discuss middle age in terms of the family they might have had." In contrast, men get their cues from the outside world —a better job, perhaps, and the prestige and respect that go with it; the point at which younger men begin to ask for advice; a realization that long-held goals had been gained or missed.

Beyond such cues, the internal and external events of middle age can be difficult to spot. Daniel Levinson of Yale, after embarking upon a four-year study of the stages of adult life, found midlife most baffling. "What it is to live through the middle years," he wrote, "is one of the best-kept secrets of our society, and perhaps in human history in general. Most persons at that age have trouble talking about it with their peers or with youth. When people learn that I am studying midlife development they frequently exhibit a kind of fascination, an awed feeling that I am trying to penetrate the impenetrable."

Part of this feeling of impenetrability arises within the very sciences of human behavior. Some scientists see midlife as principally a time of normal and productive gear-changing in goals and activities—a time of increased authority, skill and responsibility at the job, of increased security at home. In this view, the momentous events at this period are not those of a critical, clearly defined period but those that occur out of normal sequence in life—a late birth, perhaps, or an early retirement.

The difficulty of analyzing middle age is compounded by the fact that its nature changes from place to place and even from generation to generation. In a country subject to rapid and devastating upheavals, these changes can be both awesome and bewildering. Hugo Schmale,

New attitudes at forty

Priorities and interests shift gradually between the ages of 40 and 60 *(shaded areas below)*. Satisfaction with marriage begins to climb again in the forties after having sagged to its lowest level in the middle thirties, according to Roger L. Gould's analysis of a group spanning ages 16 to 60. Career mobility, which is almost taken for granted before 40, seems to be progressively less attainable in the middle years. By contrast, interest in an active social life reaches its maximum then.

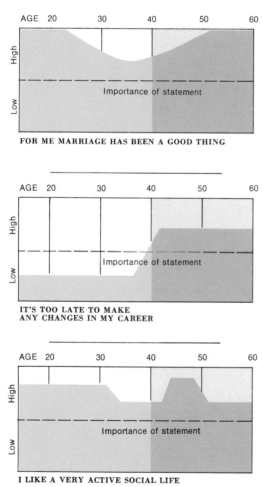

FOR ME MARRIAGE HAS BEEN A GOOD THING

IT'S TOO LATE TO MAKE
ANY CHANGES IN MY CAREER

I LIKE A VERY ACTIVE SOCIAL LIFE

head of the psychology department at Hamburg University, described a German in his middle years in the 1950s as a man or woman whose life had been shattered by World War II, and who was desperately trying to gain a new career and family foothold. In the 1960s, buoyed by economic success, those in middle age had a momentum that may have made them almost oblivious of the aging process. Schmale rounded out this record of change by noting that a middle-aged German of the 1970s was someone "who has learned to count on and cope with the insecurities of the current situation"—and then proceeded to complicate the story by pointing out that Germans do not, in any case, draw a sharp distinction between young adulthood and middle age. Even the term for middle age—*das Erwachsenealter* (literally, mature adult)—crops up only rarely in scientific literature on the life cycle and, though studies of youth and old age abound, Schmale recalled not a single German book on the subject of middle age in recent years.

Elsewhere, the meaning of midlife is obscured by other factors. In villages of India and China that still follow traditional patterns, one of the crucial events of the period in the Western world—the moment when children marry and go off to start their own homes and families—simply does not happen. There, sons live with their wives and rear their children in the parental home, as part of an extended family. In a different way, a shorter life expectancy can make the problems of middle age seem negligible. Brazil, for example, is a country in which only 19 per cent of the population is over the age of 40; in the United States, the corresponding figure is 36 per cent. Naturally enough, Brazilian scientists do not set a high priority upon the study of middle age. Vladia Weyne, a psychologist specializing in midlife problems in Rio de Janeiro, found herself the first scientist in the city to do so. "When I was writing my master's thesis," she said, "the only bibliography I could find on the subject referred to other countries: Argentina, the United States, France. There's nothing on the problem in Brazil."

When low life expectancy combines with poverty, middle age almost seems to disappear as a stage of the life cycle. For most of human history and in much of the world today, only a tiny segment of any population has ever lived beyond the age of 40. And when a man or woman must labor unceasingly for sheer survival, very little seems to happen between the beginning of adulthood and old age. Significantly, middle age is the only stage of adult life that has nothing comparable to the puberty rites of adolescence, the rites of marriage and the first child in early adulthood, and the funeral rite that brings old age to its end; the great rites of passage that celebrate the life cycle have never been de-

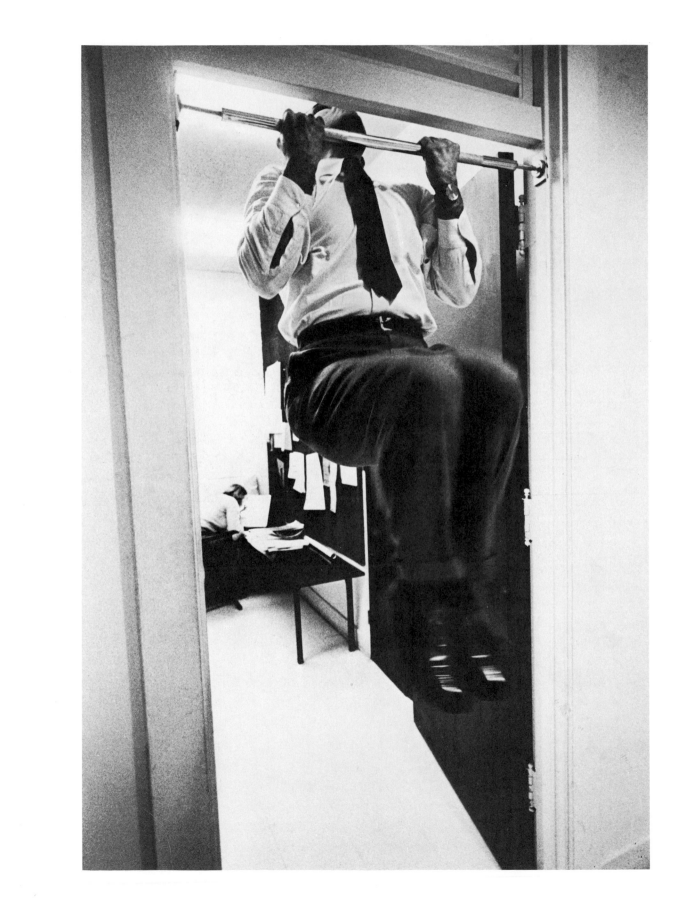

veloped for midlife. Although it is one of the momentous turning points
of life for many people, it has in the past been so limited that there was
no need to honor it with a tradition.

There is one turning point at midlife that cannot be ignored in any culture, but it applies only to women. A middle-aged woman observes her
own rite of passage with a physical change: the menopause, marking
the completion of her childbearing years. This definite and inescapable
end to fertility is a peculiarly human event; among all mammals, only
the human female and the cow elephant outlive the years of childbearing. But the menopause is only one noticeable factor in a whole cluster
of physical changes, called the climacteric, that is now known to overtake women, and in some respects may overtake men, in their middle
years. Some symptoms of the climacteric are clearly initiated by declining production of certain sex hormones; others are suspected to stem
from the hormones themselves. Associated with these physical changes
may be pronounced alterations in behavior and outlook. Those with
clear-cut physical bases are universal, observed in nearly all people of
all cultures. Others seem more pronounced in certain societies, and at-
tempts to explain these differences shed light on the human psyche.

What happens inside a woman's body at the female climacteric has
finally been figured out. The menopause itself is caused by an apparently age-programed change in the ovaries, which normally respond to
hormone-borne instructions from one of the body's master control centers, the pituitary gland in the midbrain. The timer goes off; though the
pituitary continues to secrete two sex hormones—follicle stimulating
hormone (FSH) and luteinizing hormone (LH)—the ovaries no longer
respond to these hormones, and the reproductive processes slow to a
halt. As the ovaries slacken in their function, so does the release of ripe
egg cells. Eventually, no egg cells at all travel to the uterus to lie in its
wall for possible fertilization. At the same time the lining of the uterus
no longer thickens with extra blood cells, and menstruation, in which
this blood-rich lining is sloughed off about once a month, becomes ir-
regular and eventually stops altogether.

At about the time that the ovaries slacken in the production of ripe
egg cells, they also do something else: they reduce their secretion of the
two female sex hormones called estrogen and progesterone. And the estrogen decline brings on its own set of physical symptoms, which in extent and in influence on behavior are greater than those of the
menopause. It is estrogen lack—not, as most people assume, the menopause—that causes the "hot flash," a spell of warmth, flushing and
perspiration occurring when the body's temperature-regulating system,

usually monitored by estrogen, goes temporarily haywire. The discomfort of such an episode can be compounded by embarrassment when it occurs in public. "When I would get my flashes at work, I was sure everyone could tell what was happening," said a 51-year-old woman, who then echoed the common misconception about the cause: "I felt as if I were wearing a label that said, 'Woman in Menopause.' "

Though the hot flash may provide the most dramatic sign of the climacteric, other changes are longer lasting and deeper in their effects. Estrogen helps keep the breasts firm and the skin supple; when the level of the hormone drops, breasts become flabby, skin sags and wrinkles, pouches appear under the eyes. Bones lose calcium, and backache sets in. With decreased estrogen, the lining of the vagina may become dry and rigid, making urination and sexual intercourse uncomfortable. Because estrogen keeps down the level of fats in the blood, its loss increases the risk of heart attack. Among the physical symptoms, a recurrent "lump in the throat" is caused by spasms of the esophagus, resulting from estrogen deficiency.

Both the menopause and the other events of the climacteric also cause changes in a woman's attitudes and, in subtle ways, in her emotional make-up as well. Partly because the menopause involves a woman's genital organs, it has given rise to the myth that it can and does affect sexual activity as well as menstruation and fertility. Some women, indeed, believe that the menopause means the end of love-making—and so do some men. Normally, this idea is simply not true, and women who have passed through the menopause know it is not true. Menopause affects only the reproductive system; sexual functions form part of a separate system in the body. While childbearing terminates fairly abruptly, sexual enjoyment can continue as long as a woman is healthy. If anything, the end of anxiety over an unwanted pregnancy enhances sexual pleasure; a large-scale survey of European women, published in the 1970s, found more than two thirds of them agreeing that "The menopause means love-making is less worrying."

The same European study also revealed some lesser known but fascinating facts about attitudes toward the menopause in different nations. Among other things, its findings show that while the menopause is universal, dictated as it is by the biological clocks in women's bodies, the psychological response to menopause is largely determined by culture. The conclusion is based upon extended interviews with 2,000 women, all between the ages of 46 and 55, in Great Britain, France, Belgium, West Germany and Italy. Analyzing interviews with these women, the researchers discovered that even in the obscure and intimate area of

What menopause means

When 2,000 middle-aged women in five countries were polled on attitudes toward menopause, the answers *(below)* varied with the country. To Belgian and Italian women menopause signaled old age; British women, typically unflappable, were not concerned about the change of life.

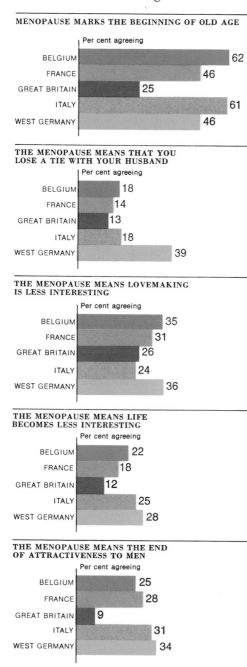

MENOPAUSE MARKS THE BEGINNING OF OLD AGE

Per cent agreeing

BELGIUM 62
FRANCE 46
GREAT BRITAIN 25
ITALY 61
WEST GERMANY 46

THE MENOPAUSE MEANS THAT YOU LOSE A TIE WITH YOUR HUSBAND

Per cent agreeing

BELGIUM 18
FRANCE 14
GREAT BRITAIN 13
ITALY 18
WEST GERMANY 39

THE MENOPAUSE MEANS LOVEMAKING IS LESS INTERESTING

Per cent agreeing

BELGIUM 35
FRANCE 31
GREAT BRITAIN 26
ITALY 24
WEST GERMANY 36

THE MENOPAUSE MEANS LIFE BECOMES LESS INTERESTING

Per cent agreeing

BELGIUM 22
FRANCE 18
GREAT BRITAIN 12
ITALY 25
WEST GERMANY 28

THE MENOPAUSE MEANS THE END OF ATTRACTIVENESS TO MEN

Per cent agreeing

BELGIUM 25
FRANCE 28
GREAT BRITAIN 9
ITALY 31
WEST GERMANY 34

menopause, the traditional idea of a "national character" apparently has real validity.

Consider, for example, the bit of folk wisdom that labels the British people as unflappable and optimistic. With regard to the menopause, at least, British women are exactly that. When asked whether the menopause "marks the beginning of old age," over 60 per cent of the Belgian and Italian women agreed that it does; in Britain, the figure was only 25 per cent. Three times as many West Germans as British—39 per cent to 13—felt that the menopause "means you lose a tie with your husband" (American women, according to a comparable study, reacted like the Germans). When West German and British women were asked whether the menopause "means the end of attractiveness to men," the contrast was even more startling: 34 per cent of the West Germans agreed that it did, only 9 per cent of the British.

More subtle than such variations and shifts of attitude are effects upon psychological balance and emotions. That some such influence does exist is unquestionable—but here again, as in the matter of sexual capability, myths outnumber facts. In a study of American women by Bernice Neugarten, over half the subjects agreed that "Women worry about losing their minds during the menopause." For many years, psychiatrists considered a psychosis called involutional melancholia to be a disturbance restricted to middle-aged women and due to the shrinking of the female reproductive organs. Today they know that involutional melancholia has nothing to do with the menopause in particular or the climacteric in general (and is not limited to women).

Once the myths are cleared away, the real psychological effects of the climacteric remain—and they are serious enough in themselves. Their expressions are well known. In an apparently reasonable discussion with a husband or a friend, one woman bursts into a fit of uncontrollable weeping. Another complains of insomnia or disturbed sleep. When a husband mildly criticizes his dinner, a wife flings her fork to the table and leaves the room in fury. Still another woman may find herself dithering for hours over the simplest decisions, paralyzed by uncertainty and a loss of self-confidence.

Behind the crying spells, anxiety and tension may lie depression that cannot be shaken off easily. According to psychoanalyst Helene Deutsch, "almost every woman in the climacterium goes through a shorter or longer period of depression."

One physician combined his experience with several patients into a composite 49-year-old he called Marcia. Until she began to suffer from insomnia, hot flashes, sudden headaches and heart palpitations, she had

been a happily married, well-adjusted woman, with three children and a husband she loved. But now there were times when an unshakable gloom seized her. She felt unneeded; her childbearing years were over, and she was afraid she would never seem attractive to her husband again and that they would no longer be able to enjoy sexual relations.

Even when she was not depressed, she often felt a great lassitude, which was so overpowering that it became hard for her to do anything. At other times she was so easily upset that it set the whole family on edge. One night, her husband came home from work and mixed drinks for her and himself, and they sat down for a quiet time together. They talked pleasantly for a while, and then he innocently asked her when dinner was going to be served. She burst into tears. Another time they were going over some bills and her husband asked about the price of a dress she had bought. She got up, stalked out of the house slamming the door behind her, and went off into the night for over an hour.

*Old age comes early for athletes,
who must perform at the peak of physical
fitness. Here a stunned and bleeding
Y. A. Tittle, veteran quarterback for the
New York Giants, kneels on the field after
a bruising tackle, realizing that his days
as a professional football player
are numbered. This game took place on
September 20, 1964, a month short of
Tittle's 38th birthday. He played out the
season, but it was to be his last.*

Since such disturbances have now been linked to hormone imbalance, they can be alleviated by estrogen treatment. Administered with the caution that must be accorded any powerful medication, it eliminates the hot flashes and backaches of the climacteric and relieves such symptoms as depression and hot temper. It is so effective that by the mid-1970s more than seven million women in the United States alone were taking hormone pills regularly to help them through the discomforts of the climacteric.

Yet it is not simply hormones that make a woman's middle years troublesome. She must face pressures and conflicts that aggravate the effects of internal biological change—or may indeed be a principal cause of the psychological and emotional distress associated with the biological change. There is the possibility of serious illness, greater now than at any time since infancy. The care of aging parents places a greater burden on middle-aged daughters and daughters-in-law than on sons and sons-in-law. The middle-aged wife may have to cope with a husband undergoing his own midlife transition.

And specifically feminine is what has come to be called the empty nest syndrome. The ending of fertility at the menopause may be a devastating shock to a woman whose self-esteem depended substantially upon her ability to bear and nurture children. At or about this time, her self-esteem receives another blow. The children she has nurtured leave her home, and their dependency upon her diminishes or disappears. The problem of filling time can be acute. Said one woman: "My husband and I were actually embarrassed with one another. We hadn't been alone together for twenty-five years. There didn't seem to be anything to do, any reason for cooking or caring, nothing to talk about."

Purposeful activity seems to make a big difference in the ease with which a woman passes these years, according to an internist whose patients had, at different stages in his career, included both housewives and professional women. "When I was in private practice, seeing mainly middle-class homemakers," he said, "complaints about the climacteric were common. I rarely hear them now that I have joined a corporate staff, and most of my women patients are working at demanding, satisfying jobs." His observation is one of many suggesting that a woman's midlife may be less influenced by biology than by culture.

The fact that hormones can affect—to whatever extent—the midlife behavior of women has led many scientists to speculate that the same might be true of men. Male testes secrete a masculine sex hormone called testosterone, comparable to the estrogen secreted by a woman's ovaries. Testosterone triggers male sexual development and maintains sexual libido; it is apparently responsible for an innately male instinct of physical aggressiveness. At about the age of 40, its production begins to decrease—not rapidly and dramatically, like the decrease of estrogen in women, but in a slowly declining curve that will run to the end of a man's life. This decline, some specialists believe, may be involved in the physical and emotional changes that strike men in the middle years. Some are, like a woman's menopause, obvious and long recognized. Others are only now being considered as part of a cluster of symptoms.

Certain physical facts about the middle years of a man's life are, like the climacteric in women, universal. Men are intensely conscious of these facts. When Bernice Neugarten studied awareness of middle age, she noted that "Health changes are more of an age marker for men than for women. . . . Women refer much less frequently to biological changes and to concern over health." Both men and women may resort to what Neugarten calls "body monitoring"—protective strategies designed to keep a failing middle-aged body at a stable level of appearance and performance. But American men, contrary to general opinion, go to greater lengths than women do. While women may diet and experiment with cosmetics, men do that and more, often adopting wigs and undertaking such strenuous exercise as jogging a mile every morning. Moreover, they may be pressed to such efforts by their wives, for women, according to Neugarten's findings, "are more concerned over the body-monitoring of their husbands than of themselves." For men, the strategies for body-monitoring reflect "a new sense of physical vulnerability." This sense of vulnerability, bringing with it feelings of insecurity and even of impotence, is of course justified. The kidneys and digestive system do not work as well as they used to, and coronary failure, the greatest killer at this age, becomes a worrisome possibility. Novelist Josh Greenfeld wrote of feeling a sharp pain in his chest one night. After suffering in silence for a time, he told his wife—and she immediately called his doctor. "Don't worry," the doctor said, "your husband isn't overweight and he's still in his thirties." "No, no, he isn't," cried Greenfeld's wife, "he's over forty." "In that case," the doctor snapped, "I'll meet him at the hospital in fifteen minutes."

Such physical debilities are the inevitable result of aging. They eventually strike every man everywhere, and they raise more or less the same kinds of concerns. But some men are also affected at this time by other changes that are less obviously physical in origin. It is these changes that some authorities now trace to declines in hormonal levels, for the symptoms mirror those of the female climacteric. Whether they actually represent a male climacteric or not, they undeniably exist.

Somewhere between 40 and 60, men may exhibit unusual nervousness, irritability, depression and indecisiveness. What is more, say many students of the midlife years, there may be extended periods of disturbance and upheaval accompanied by sustained feelings of helplessness and futility. Some men seem to focus upon the emptiness of their own achievements, rather than the satisfaction and value they represent; on the strains of marriage rather than its delights and securities; on the decline of health and the inevitability of death rather than the many years of reasonably good health and productivity that lie ahead. At worst, these fears and preoccupations can lead to profound changes of outlook and to an often painful reassessment that has been termed the midlife crisis.

Many men never seem to undergo this crisis, either in their behavior or in their own conceptions of themselves. What is more interesting is the entire absence of the midlife crisis in many parts of the world. Indeed, the most striking fact about the crisis may be the nature of the culture in which it does or does not appear. In some primitive societies it cannot occur, simply because men die too young to experience it. In others men live through midlife into old age but do not seem to encounter a stage of crisis along the way. In modern industrialized societies, on the other hand, the midlife crisis does turn up but in a strange pattern of distribution. Psychologists and sociologists in Germany and France, for example, see few signs of it; in England, it is becoming increasingly common; and in the United States, where it is apparently most widespread, it has inspired study in more than half a dozen institutions.

Why these disparities? Part of the answer may lie in the extent to which personal attitudes change in the adult years. Anthropologists and sociologists agree that industrial and urban societies favor such change, while primitive and rural ones inhibit it. In this view, the United States may be an extreme toward which all modern societies are moving—and America may be getting more extreme all the time, with a corresponding rise in the frequency of the midlife crisis. Says sociologist Orville Brim Jr.: "In primitive, slow-changing environments there is likely to be continuity in personality, but in the United States, where both work and family situations are in rapid alteration, life-span personality change may be increasing . . . and continuity of personality increasingly difficult to demonstrate."

Describing one of these two poles, Sol Wirth of the University of Pennsylvania writes of the psychological stability encouraged by the prospects of a middle-aged man among the Navajo Indians: "At 45 . . .

the Navajo is stepping into a new hierarchy. Now he is a leader. He doesn't have to perform. His children and grandchildren can ride the horses and climb the mountains and be virile. He does other things better, like giving advice and orders. If we're talking about climacteric depression as a biocultural event, it doesn't appear to exist here."

In contrast, the midlife man of industrialized society faces a series of dismaying jolts to his self-esteem and emotional balance—the conscious loss of youth in a culture that prizes youth, the inevitable gap between aspiration and authority. In America today, the consequences erupt savagely in clinical statistics. Illnesses often considered psychosomatic rise sharply: peptic ulcers, for example, occur most frequently between the ages of 40 and 50. Infidelity, often an expression of sexual uncertainty and despair, increases; as far back as the 1950s Alfred Kinsey reported that it reached a peak by the early forties. Some men simply run away from it all—an estimated 100,000 middle-class, middle-aged men leave home every year (although in 1974 it was reported that more American wives left home than husbands). Suicide, which is in one sense an extreme form of running away at this age, climbs alarmingly. It reaches a rate of just under 105 per 100,000 men in the 40-to-59 age group, roughly three times the rate for males who are between 15 and 24 years old.

The midlife crisis—in those few areas and cultures in which it does appear—is normally survived and surpassed. And in the years that follow—perhaps 15 or more before old age—the rewards of midlife can be savored. In most cases, it is a time of peace, security and satisfaction for both men and women—and with good reason. With the children grown and gone, a husband and wife can settle down to a life of fewer responsibilities and greater ease. Social activities increase, and both daily life and leisure are quite literally enriched: family income peaks when the heads of the family are between 45 and 54 years old—the very years when they are likely to pay off their mortgage and complete the last big expense of educating their children. They may have worked up the ladder on the job, or found new and more satisfying careers or at least come to enjoy the security and privileges of the veteran. Some men and women achieve the secure status of leaders, almost like the elders of simpler societies. Instead of competing, such a person, as Theodore Lidz puts it, "need no longer prove himself from day to day, for he is credited with past accomplishments."

In this atmosphere of ease and respect, midlife can become an age of acceptance. One man said, "I feel a weakening of the need to be a great man and an increasing feeling of, 'Let's just get through this the best way we can. Never mind hitting any home runs; let's just get through the ball game without being beaned.' "

Yet there is more than acceptance once the midlife crisis has passed, for people often feel a new pride in their capacities and abilities. In Bernice Neugarten's study of middle age, both men and women spoke of a new authority and autonomy in their lives, of knowing what would work in most situations and what would not, of transcending the trial-and-error methods of youth and young adulthood. She concluded, "The successful middle-aged person often describes himself as no longer 'driven,' but as now the 'driver'—in short, 'in command.' "

In the woman, particularly, the sense of mastery is often enhanced by a new-found sense of freedom. "She is still young enough," points out Theodore Lidz, "to start on a new career, re-enter an old one, or devote herself more fully to some activity she had pursued part-time while occupied with her children." Some men may even envy their wives a bit

The deep black worn by these middle-aged Spanish country women signifies something more than mourning for departed husbands and other relatives. Anthropologists say the solemn garb means that the women who wear it have reached the point in life where they are no longer concerned with physical beauty and with being attractive to men.

at this period; a wife may be finding fresh rewards at just the moment her husband is settling into the last stages of his career. But men as well as women can subscribe to a statement on middle-age freedom by Wellesley College President Barbara Newell, even though she was speaking for and to women when she made it. A woman in her forties, she said, "begins to be much more sure of her tastes and interests. One has explored many options and begins to focus, which in itself frees time and frees emotional energies for pursuits that have particular meaning."

The path from the midlife crisis to this sense of mastery and freedom may be long and hard—but according to Yale's Daniel Levinson, it is only part of the story. In working out patterns of development for all the adult years, Levinson places the roots of a man's midlife crisis in his thirties, when he may make his last great choices *(Chapter 3)* by bidding for success in his own field or by striking out into a new career, or even by changing his goals and purposes entirely. He enters upon a midlife transition, "a turning point or boundary region between two periods of greater stability." During this period the crisis can occur. When it is concluded, it resolves itself in a process Levinson labels restabilization: The midlife transition ends and a new life structure is begun.

The new structure may assume any of several forms. A man may settle happily at an already achieved level of security and success—the same marriage, the same job and the same life style, but with a sense of reconciliation and fulfillment missing in the preceding years. He may change careers, calling upon inner resources that have been dormant. Or, in rare cases, he may find himself for the first time and fulfill a purpose in life totally different from that previously expected, adopting a course with no real connection to jobs and earning a living.

Perhaps the best way to grasp this intricate scheme of stages and choices is to follow one of Levinson's case histories in detail. In a man who followed the second of the three paths described above, the great choice burst upon him with explosive force. A millionaire executive by his mid-thirties, he determined to do what he had always dreamed of doing: write a novel. Abandoning his business at the age of 37, he set to work at his typewriter. Eventually his novel was submitted for publication, published and modestly praised.

Now he entered a characteristic waiting period of uncertainty and indecision. Ill at ease in his new life, the executive-turned-novelist doggedly struggled through the next few years in a kind of maddening career schizophrenia. For one year, he not only worked at his writing but also taught creative writing part time at a university. Later, thinking semi-isolation might help him to concentrate, he moved his working

continued on page 119

FROM SUBURBIA TO PARIS' LEFT BANK

FROM PRIESTHOOD TO FATHERHOOD

FROM SELLING TO WALRUS HUNTING

FROM HIGH SOCIETY TO POLITICS

Changing course in midlife

At the age of 48, John DeLorean apparently had everything going for him. A vice president of General Motors, at a salary of $550,000, he was living in affluence in a suburb of Detroit and was in line for the presidency of GM, one of the world's richest and most powerful corporations. Abruptly he quit his job and took an unsalaried position as head of a voluntary group engaged in persuading corporations to hire disadvantaged people.

DeLorean's act is a spectacular example of a phenomenon increasingly common among people of middle age. Coming to the midpoint in life, they re-assess their jobs and life styles, find them wanting and decide to do something about their dissatisfaction. They turn their backs on nearly everything they have known before and veer off into totally new careers and strikingly different ways of life. Their numbers include both sexes, and people in all kinds of occupations.

On these pages are a salesman, a countess, a priest and an editor who made the midlife switch. Each one of them took up an existence that contrasted sharply with the past, and each found satisfaction and a sense of fulfillment in his new way of life.

A FULLER LIFE IN PARIS

An expatriate in a Paris apartment, widower Stuart Troup plays a spirited game of chess with son David, who is 11 years old, under the kibitzing eye of daughter Laura, 12. Troup had been a successful editor of the Long Island newspaper *Newsday,* but when his wife died he decided to move to Europe with his children to seek what he terms "a more humane life."

After two years in Rome scrabbling to earn a living as a freelance writer, he settled in Paris' Left Bank, working as a newspaper editor for *The International Herald Tribune.* Says Troup: "Our lives are a little fuller and more pleasant in Europe."

A DIFFERENT SOCIAL COMMITMENT

A former Dutch Catholic priest, Dolf Coppes, shares an intimate moment with his wife and young daughters in his home outside Amsterdam. Coppes agrees with the views of other Dutch priests who in recent years have militantly challenged the rule of priestly celibacy. In 1965, at the age of 40, Coppes left the church to marry a Protestant nurse.

Coppes did not cut himself off entirely from his pastoral connections. For a while he was a secular priest, well known for his sermons on Catholic radio and television programs. He became involved with an interfaith group later and preached ecumenically in local churches. In 1972 he became a member of the Dutch Parliament at The Hague.

PEACE OF MIND ON THE TUNDRA

Former salesman Jack Fuller rests his dog team during a lonely ride on the frozen Bering Sea. When Fuller turned 40 years old in 1962, he was earning a comfortable income, selling graduation caps and gowns in Ohio and providing his wife and two young daughters with the conventional amenities. But he felt that he had not done what he really wanted to do: go to Alaska. His wife also wanted to give up the suburban life, but her goal was the Virgin Islands.

The couple agreed to try Alaska first and have lived there ever since. Fuller is now a battalion commander in the National Guard and his wife teaches school. They have settled in to their new life and want little else. "Being alone in all that vastness," says Fuller, "is like being closer to God."

A CHALLENGE IN PUBLIC SERVICE

Susanna Agnelli was born rich and privileged, the granddaughter of Italy's great automobile maker, Giovanni Agnelli, who founded the famous Fiat autoworks. She married a count, raised six children and divided her time between the dual roles of high-society wife and mother. The plebian business of local politics was remote from her sphere.

Countess Agnelli's marriage turned sour, middle age came on, her children went their separate ways, and she decided she needed a change. She found a challenge close to home. In the area surrounding the Tuscan town of Monte Argentario, where she lived, ugly housing developments were springing up, and she became actively involved in an effort to preserve the natural beauty of the region.

She was elected to the town council, served four years and then was chosen mayor of Monte Argentario. Her second career enabled her to spend her days listening to the problems of the townspeople, poking about the harbor and talking to boat repairmen *(right)*, fighting the encroachments of the developers and enjoying her new life.

quarters to a cabin in the woods—but there he soon ran across a promising tract of land and, almost by force of habit, bought and sold it, adding more to his impressive bank account. Still unsatisfied—as he explained it, what he wanted to do always seemed somehow different from what he ended up doing—he returned to the city. There, at the urging of a publisher but after much hesitation, he agreed to give up fiction for a time to work on a series of historical books.

At this point, in his forties, the transition engulfed him in midlife crisis—and, by extension, his family as well. A few months after his return to the city, as he continued to agonize over the meaning and direction of his life, one of his children developed erratic behavior in school as a result of family conflicts. Soon afterward the writer entered psychotherapy, along with his wife and son. With the help of the family therapist, he focused upon the immediate problems that tortured him: Had he failed as a husband and father? How much did he really want to write novels? At the same time, he began to explore deeper issues: Was he tough enough to follow the new career he had chosen—or was he, in some paradoxical way, too tough? In fact, what kind of person was he, really; and how could he become more complete?

Gradually, he came to realize that one of the problems he faced arose from his relationship with his wife. She had not particularly wanted him to be a writer; if anything, she had preferred him as a businessman. But as he came to see both her and himself more realistically, he realized he did not have to live up to the masculine image she had formed of him; he could allow gentler, more nurturing and more creative elements of his personality to emerge. Having learned this much, he was able to decide at last what he wanted. He told his wife, in effect: Whether you approve or not, I am going to put writing at the center of my life and keep it there; whatever you want to share of my life is what I want to share with you. It was a decision his wife could endorse. His midlife crisis was ending and the next phase of their life together, a time of restabilization and creative growth, was beginning.

Few passages through the midlife transition are as intense and uncomfortable as this one, and few restabilizations are as hard-won. Even rarer is the final possibility that Levinson suggests beyond the transition —the possibility that, at midlife, an individual may find his true calling for the first time, not so much in a second career as in a symbolic rebirth. Yet such cases do occur. Mahatma Gandhi, for example, reached his own midlife as a fumbling, unsuccessful attorney at law. Armed with a degree from London's Inns of Court and sporting the stiff clothes and correct manners of the British middle class, he tried at least three

times to set up a law practice in India and South Africa—and failed every time. Then, after a painful time of introspection and indecision, he turned his back on Western ways and was born to a new life as a dedicated political and spiritual leader of the Indian people and a prophet of a peculiarly Indian philosophy of nonviolence.

The psychoanalyst Erik Erikson has tried to account for such profound reversals of intent and direction as the midlife turmoil is ended. In Erikson's scheme of the life cycle, a great internal choice is made at midlife, comparable to the basic decisions of earlier years. A midlife crisis missed or fumbled leads to stagnation, a state in which an individual's essential vitality sinks too low for further development. But if the crisis is confronted and resolved, it can lead to enormous gains in perspective and creativity. The greatest gain of all, says Erikson, is generativity, which he defines as a concern for and commitment to the next generation of mankind.

Few men have expressed this midlife commitment better than an American named Meriwether Lewis. Today, Lewis seems to have been young, not middle-aged, when he underwent this transformation of purpose—but he seemed middle-aged to himself. In the America of his time, the beginning of the 19th Century, only one man in 10 lived beyond the age of 45—by a twist of fate, Lewis himself would be dead within five years—and he had tried a reasonably wide variety of careers. In the military, he had risen to the rank of captain; later, he had embarked on government service as secretary to President Thomas Jefferson. Now Jefferson was sending him out on a new venture, as explorer of the unknown lands that stretched to the Pacific. On Sunday, August 18, 1805, encamped on an unnamed mountaintop in the raw Western wilderness, Lewis scribbled these words in his diary:

"This day I completed my thirty-first year, and conceived that I had in all human probability now existed about half the period which I am to remain in this sublunary world. I reflected that I had as yet done but little, very little, indeed, to further the happiness of the human race, or to advance the information of the succeeding generation. I viewed with regret the many hours I have spent in indolence and now soarly feel the want of that information which those hours would have given me had they been judiciously expended. But since they are past and cannot be recalled, I dash from me the gloomy thought and resolve in the future to redouble my exertions and at least endeavor to promote those two primary objects of human existence by giving them the aid of that portion of talents which nature and fortune have bestowed on me; or in the future to live *for mankind* as I have heretofore lived *for myself.*"

Special towns for the aging

Ethel and Walter Nelson enjoy sitting on the patio of their retirement home in Seal Beach to read, do crossword puzzles and sip coffee with their parakeet between them. A laconic former chief engineer on oil tankers, he said shortly after moving to the age-segregated retirement village: "We like it fine."

Today the stages in life may be marked less by formal rites of passage than by moves from one home to another. None of these shifts in residence is likely to be more poignant than the one that follows the middle years. The children have grown up and moved away. Many friends and neighbors are gone. The old house, scene of so much laughter and tears, is too big to care for and too lonely to live in.

More and more societies now provide special housing for those whose family and work responsibilities have largely ended. Sweden pioneered such housing in the early 1960s with the first government-sponsored apartment complexes, which now house some 60,000 people, aged 60 and over. In the Netherlands 8 per cent of the elderly inhabit special housing, and France has some of the world's most self-sufficient communities for retired workers.

The American innovation is retirement villages—entire towns built for older people. The first, Sun City in Arizona, grew to 34,000 inhabitants in 15 years. It was soon followed by many similar communities, one of which, Seal Beach, near Los Angeles, was photographed by LIFE in 1963 at the end of the town's second year.

Yet only one retired person in 10 can afford to live in one of these villages. And the organized life, isolated from the young, repels many. But studies such as that by psychologist Susan Sherman in California show that those who have chosen age-segregated communities like them and stay. For people who are joiners, who want to keep busy among friends their age, a retirement village provides pleasurable surroundings for the autumn of life.

Women in a reducing class hold a meeting. Anyone who has gained weight during the week must wear a sign saying she is "a pig" (left).

A concern for keeping healthy

Among the greatest appeals of communities for older people are, understandably, facilities for guarding health. At Seal Beach a reducing class *(above)* helps women to trim off unwelcome, and medically dangerous, extra pounds. Exercise is popular—especially cycling on easy-to-handle tricycles.

In case of illness, Seal Beach has a well-equipped medical clinic with visiting nurses and doctors on call 24 hours a day. But a major complaint about many other retirement villages has been a failure to provide such facilities or even to plan the communities so elderly people can live comfortably in them.

Pedaling her "adultrike," Mrs. Belle Smith carries groceries home from the village's supermarket. Other ways to exercise are offered by a golf course, swimming pools and shuffleboard courts.

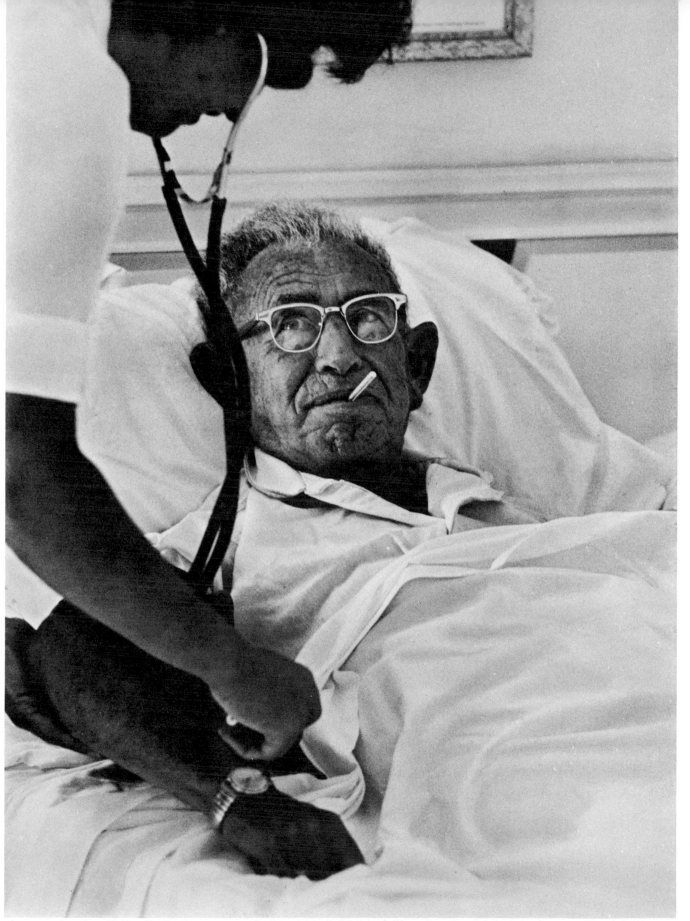

A nurse takes Sam Helfond's blood pressure and temperature in his home. Though an invalid, he joined many village clubs.

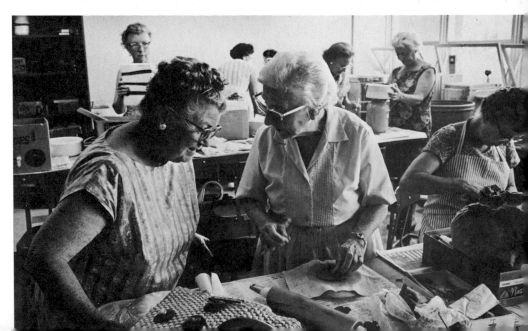

George Yeomans builds a desk in one of several workshops. Determined to occupy his time, Yeomans signed up for dancing classes and weekend dances, saying: "Age is a state of mind and I don't believe in keeping a record of birthdays. I'm over the hill but I'm still going."

Women mold clay at a ceramics class. The products of such classes are often sold and the proceeds donated to charity; the fact that the work is useful satisfies a psychological need for many reared in America's work ethic.

The recreations of the retired

Free classes in arts and crafts, such as carpentry and ceramics *(left)*, plus lessons in painting, bridge, and ballroom and square dancing are only a few of the programs organized to maintain purposeful activity for people who no longer have much they really must do.

Residents formed an orchestra and a variety of choral groups, and put on elaborate shows *(pages 130-131)*. In all, there are around 200 clubs, ranging from pinochle players to a group that discusses United States foreign policy. The busy schedules provide a sense of purpose for men who are used to working, and they help the women by getting their husbands out of the house.

Hal Smith pounds the piano as his neighbors sing lustily. The community sing is a popular feature every Monday evening. Favored songs are such standbys as "My Wild Irish Rose" and "Let Me Call You Sweetheart."

Harper Perry chats quietly with his grandchildren, who live nearby and often visit him.

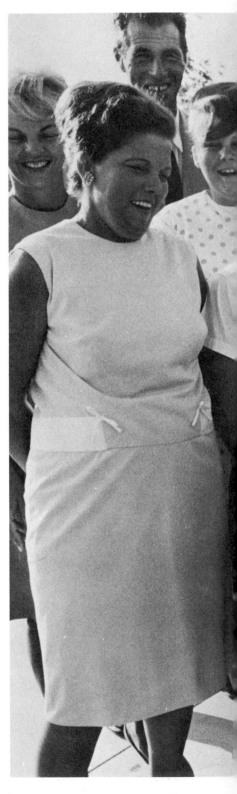

Back in the bosom of the family

Many older people congregate to avoid living with, and being a burden on, children. Nevertheless, brief family visits are glorious occasions that last just long enough for everybody to enjoy seeing the others, but not long enough to wear the old people out.

The get-togethers may be a simple reunion of a grandfather, such as Harper Perry *(above)*, a retired oil field driller, with loving grandchildren. Or they may be a gathering of the clans to celebrate the wedding of two residents, such as that of widower Henry McKinley and widow Genevieve Daugherty *(right)*, who decided to be married after a four-month courtship.

Laughing newlyweds Henry and Genevieve McKinley are ringed by their 17 children and grandchildren, some of them his, some hers.

With a youthful bounce displayed by many residents of Seal Beach, the chorus line of the Follies (average age 58 1/2) hoofs it like seasoned troupers. The Follies, which packs the village's 2,500-seat amphitheater, is written and staged by residents. The director, a retired actor, said that scheduling rehearsals was his biggest headache: "No one has time for anything—they're all too busy."

The Vintage Years

5

For most people in the industrialized world the last stage of life begins with a bump: retirement. Like it or not they are abruptly detached from the work force, patted on the back for a job well done and handed a passport to the country of the old. "That's all there is," they are told. "We'll take it from here. You can go now. Enjoy your old age."

Retirement is so common today that it is generally regarded as a natural rite of passage, like birth, marriage or death, and the 65th birthday is considered the threshold of old age. In the United States 86 per cent of all those over 65 were out of the work force in 1974; in Japan the figure was 69 per cent, in France, 91.5 per cent; and in Italy, 94.3 per cent. This abrupt transition takes place at about 65 years of age even though old-age pensions may become available sooner (in Japan, for example, women retire at 55 and men at 60) and even though, on the other hand, many employers permit workers to postpone retirement. But the abrupt severance from work is in fact arbitrary. There is no magic in the number 65 or any other specified age, no programed event in the life cycle that automatically changes people at this age the way puberty changes them around 12 or 13. Most 65-year-olds are not old in the sense of physical or mental decrepitude. As a group, in much of the world, they can look forward to an average 15 more years of life and 10 more of good health. They could go right on working, and many, like the German farm couple wistfully studying their wedding picture at left, do in fact work right up to the end of their lives.

Cut off from their jobs and the mainstream of life, retired people face financial and psychological adjustments. Income is reduced, children have their own families, old friends are gone. They may feel useless and isolated and society's attitude toward them may reinforce this feeling. More than at any time since childhood they are now recognizable —and regarded—as members of a special class, although in many ways they are more diverse than younger people.

How effectively an individual will adjust to this dramatic change in his life depends on a variety of factors. Psychologists have constructed a scale of adaptability for the aging, classifying various types from the "reorganizers," who substitute new activities for the workaday ones left behind and continue busily productive lives, to the "disorganized," who become so apathetic they cannot even think clearly. What is surprising, considering the abrupt changes in everyday routine and emotional outlook involved in the transition to old age, is the relative ease with which it is generally made. The idea that withdrawal from the working world brings on a rapid decline into feeble dependence is a myth. The fact is that more and more people find the concluding cycle of life to be one of the most enjoyable of all its stages. Their numbers are increasing every day. In every country medical progress enables a greater proportion of men and women to reach the age of 65. The elderly comprise the fastest-growing segment of the world population; by 1980 there will be 57 million more people over 65 than there were in 1970. Most will be retired, and while some will miss their work, the majority will be glad to be done with toil and to savor the chance to enjoy leisure.

The idea that people should stop working while they are still in good health and proceed to live out their lives in retirement is a fairly recent innovation. For the great part of human history, and in many cultures even today, most people have worked until they dropped —and the majority dropped long before they were 65 years old. Old people were deemed an asset—perhaps because there were so few of them—and no one would have thought of asking them to retire while they were still healthy; their production, even if lessened, was needed.

But now that there are more old people around and fewer workers can supply the world's goods and services, there is no economic necessity for people to work until death or failing health makes them stop. Moreover, there are positive political and economic benefits to be gained from inducing the elderly to leave the work force with a pension. When German Chancellor Otto von Bismarck instituted the world's first comprehensive social security program in 1881, and at the same time arbitrarily established retirement age at 65, he was not concerned with the welfare of the workers. His aim was to weaken the appeal of socialism. He declared, "Whoever has a pension for his old age is far more content and far easier to handle than one who has no such prospect." Other European countries followed Germany's lead—not necessarily from the same motive—during the next few decades, but the United States resisted the idea until the Great Depression of the 1930s; then humanitarian reformers who had been urging social insurance joined forces with those who sought to relieve unemployment by removing the elderly from the competition for jobs. Together they pushed through the Social Security Act, which has since been supplemented by other governmental aid to the elderly and a proliferation of privately financed pension plans.

Bismarck's goal has been reached only partway. Whoever has a pension is more content but not always entirely content. The sudden loss of a salary check may be a major problem. In Japan pensions amount to only 35 per cent of an average worker's pay. In France the figure is 40 per cent; in Germany it is 56 per cent after working for 50 years; and in England it is 45.7 per cent for married people and 29.9 per cent for single men and women. In the United States a survey has shown that Social Security benefits and company pension payments together add up to less than 40 per cent of preretirement income for more than half the retired people. For most people, retirement is a financial blow.

Some retired people, especially those who enjoyed their work and did not want to retire, suffer additionally from loss of role and status. Suddenly they are unneeded. They have no place to go every day, no responsibilities, none of the satisfactions and psychological rewards of doing a job for which they have been trained, no renewal of the respect of their colleagues and subordinates. Marital disputes may erupt when a retired person is home all day after a lifetime of going to work. In a few extreme cases the anxieties over loss of role can bring about irritability, depression, psychosomatic illness and even early death.

These dire symptoms make up what has been called the retirement syndrome, which is supposed to strike people when they leave their jobs, bringing on a quick decline into illness, senility and the grave. "Poor Harry," mourners will say at a friend's funeral, "he'd still be alive today if only he had stayed active in the business instead of retiring." This idea is a myth. Only a small fraction of retired people fall victim to the retirement syndrome.

This conclusion was evident from a study of retirement by Cornell University researchers who followed several thousand men and women from all walks of life for seven years, interviewing them several times before and after they stopped working. The investigators found that fewer than one quarter suffered from feelings of uselessness or rolelessness, that "retirement does not cause a sudden deterioration in psychological health," and that the decline in general health seemed to be about the same for those who retired and those who continued working. In general, those who were compelled to retire against their will were less satisfied than those who retired voluntarily, but of the minor-

ity who had feared that retirement would be "unsatisfying," about half reported afterward that their fears were not realized. A similar study concluded that among unskilled blue-collar workers "earlier retirement actually may conserve health and extend life."

The most strenuous objections to retirement come from professionals and executives, who tend to like their work and enjoy the status that goes with it. Surprisingly, however, it is these upper-echelon men and women who generally adapt most easily to the loss of role once retirement takes place.

This apparent contradiction is explained by Ida Harper Simpson, a Duke University sociologist who studied the ways people of different social classes adjust to retirement. Simpson points out that professionals and executives are accustomed to organizing their own daily routines and they know how to plan their work and leisure. They are also likely to be known in their fields and to belong to several community or professional organizations that will welcome their participation. Whether they take up hobbies, plunge themselves into charity drives or continue some aspect of their careers, they have both the opportunities and the abilities to restructure their lives, and they adapt quickly to retirement.

Simpson's study indicates that middle-level clerks, salespeople, foremen and semiskilled workers often face difficult adjustment problems. Among those she studied, these people "found little intrinsic meaning in their work and looked forward to giving it up for a life of leisure, but they tend to be uncertain about what to do and how to do it," she wrote. They have little experience in planning their time and their narrower range of interests restricts their retirement choices. The kind of work they have done is also a factor. Workers who are accustomed to physical exertion might be discouraged by declining vigor from strenuous activities they would enjoy. Salespeople and foremen, who are used to dealing with people, are better off. They may find outlets in clubs and lodge activities.

All these studies illustrate the fact that retirement in the modern world has become to a considerable extent an artificial event. It need not result from any natural change, physical or psychological. Neither does it inevitably bring about physical or psychological changes. And yet it is not totally divorced from the realities of life. True retirement involves more than accepting a pension; it means withdrawal from the normal routine of the working world. When people take that step they can generally see approaching—if not already at hand—a period of marked bodily change. Active and capable they may still be, but time is running out. They are growing old.

With advancing years all living organisms deteriorate, weaken, shrivel and slow down. Whatever else may happen to an old person, his physical functions and prowess inevitably will wither away. Many scientists question the theory that biological aging is the result of environmental wear and tear on the organism. If that theory were true, they speculate, a few fortunate, well-protected individuals would live many times longer than others. Some dogs would live to the age of 50, some humans to 250. That never happens. There is not much difference in length of life between healthy individuals of a species, although there is a great variation between species. The human life span has changed little, if at all, in the 5,000 years for which there are records. Medical progress has increased life expectancy, not longevity: more individuals are able to reach the upper limit, around 100 years, but that limit is unchanged. One reason, apparently, is that death is necessary to preserve a species —only by replacing individuals can a species adapt to a changing environment. And as diseases cannot be relied on to kill everyone, the reasoning goes, the human body must be programed to self-destruct. Nature presumably equips every organism with a time clock set to

Foster grandparent Joseph Guthrie, 70, reads to one of his charges at a Head Start center in Charleston, West Virginia. Unlike volunteers in some programs, grandparents are paid: $1,670 annually.

Busy retirees: never too old to be useful

The myth of retirement as enforced idleness is disproved by some 135,000 active aging Americans, for whom the completion of one career has meant the beginning of a new one in community projects. Among them is RSVP, the Retired Senior Volunteer Program, which places those over 60 in libraries, museums and city agencies, doing part-time jobs for which their skills suit them. A more specific program utilizes the talents of former managers and administrators. Called SCORE, the Service Corps of Retired Executives, this group helps the operators of small businesses solve their problems.

No experience or technical skills are required for one of the most satisfying of retirement careers, the Foster Grandparent Program, which seeks out people who enjoy children. Its members spend 20 hours a week caring for youngsters —each of the grandparents has his own pair—in hospitals, correctional institutions or day care centers.

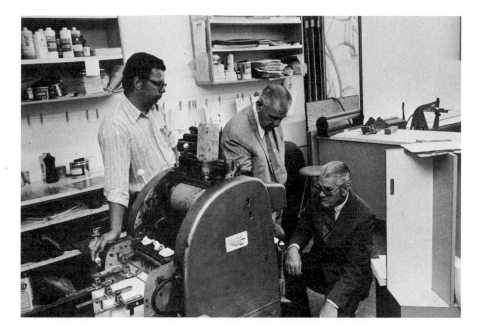

The ex-president of the General Finance Corporation, SCORE's Ray E. Titus (center), advises the owner of a copying service (left) in Fort Lauderdale, Florida, on problems encountered when the shop had to be relocated. There is no charge to the businessman for the expertise of the SCORE volunteer.

RSVP participant Theodore A. Harden, 63, a former inspector for a chemical plant, drives youngsters to a community day care center in his hometown of Staunton, Virginia, two days a week.

run down. That timer is called aging; and aging ultimately is death.

The symptoms of aging are caused by the loss or malfunction of individual cells in every organ of the body. Just why cells die is still a mystery, but Leonard Hayflick of Stanford University's School of Medicine found evidence that the life span of cells is somehow controlled from within. Lung cells from human embryos, cultured in Hayflick's laboratory, lived and divided normally—but only until they had doubled about 50 times. Then they simply ceased dividing and died, regardless of outside conditions. Hayflick found that when the cells were frozen before they reached their limit they stopped dividing, but when they thawed out again they "remembered" how many doublings they still had scheduled and went on multiplying again until they reached their limit. Cells from shorter-lived species, and cells taken from older humans, divided correspondingly fewer times before dying.

Hayflick's results are disputed by other scientists, who see somewhat different solutions to the mystery of aging. They are trying to discover whether the cells die because of "instructions" in their genetic core material, the DNA molecule, or because of errors that creep into the cell's production of protein, or whether in fact the hormonal system regulates the life span by releasing a "death hormone" that sabotages the cells.

As the cells disappear, a number of things happen. Tissues and muscles shrink, and strength and endurance fade, impairing the ability to work. Skin wrinkles and tends to get flabby as the flesh beneath it wastes away. The whole body shrinks and weight decreases. At the same time the nerves are losing cells too, so that they cannot transmit signals as accurately or as fast as they did before. Consequently, all senses weaken perceptibly, especially sight and hearing. And every organ and function —reflexes, thinking, digestion—simply slows down. (Athletes notice this general loss of speed at the age of 30; a healthy typist may not feel it until 70.) Then dark spots appear on the skin as certain cells fail to process wastes properly. Hair turns white as cells in the roots cease manufacturing pigment. Finally the coordination of the entire system breaks down because the organs are deteriorating at different rates.

Happily, two fairly common assumptions about aging turn out to be false. There is no biological imperative either for a sudden end to sexual activity or for a general intellectual decline. The overall reduction in vigor and strength may decrease sexual capacity—as it may impair the ability to run up three flights of stairs—but it does not decree a halt to sex for either men or women.

According to the principal investigators of sex, William Masters and Virginia Johnson, "Aging males usually are able to continue some form of active sexual expression into the 70- and even 80-year age groups. . . . Regularity of sexual expression is the key to sexual responsiveness for the aging male." Elderly women may reject sex, believing it is not proper after menopause. They are mistaken. "There seems to be no physiologic reason why the frequency of sexual expression found satisfactory for the younger woman should not be carried over into the postmenopausal years," said Masters and Johnson. "There is no time limit drawn by the advancing years to female sexuality."

Up until a few years ago most psychologists would have agreed that a loss of intellectual ability is an inevitable consequence of age. This belief emerged from thousands of intelligence tests given to men and women of different age groups in the 1930s, '40s and '50s. The results invariably showed that younger people performed better than their seniors, but there were several flaws in these studies. First of all, the tests themselves were originally designed to predict success in school and careers, and had so little to do with the lives and concerns of elderly people that meaningful answers could not be expected. An even more serious weakness was the attempt to pair people of different ages at the same point in time. The differences in results thus were caused not only by age changes but also by differences between generations, reflecting the fact that younger people in modern societies are better educated than their elders and have had more experience with tests.

Both these faults were eliminated in more recent investigations. The tests were administered to the same individuals over many years and were designed to be more relevant and more interesting to the elderly (problems based on using the classified section of a phone book, for example). The oldsters did much better. On the average, the difference between the performance of a man at 60 and the same man at 70 proved to be much less than the difference between a man of 70 and another man 10 years younger.

There are, however, certain areas of decline that everyone must face. They come under a heading that one psychologist called loss of speed. The disappearance of cells in the brain and the spinal cord inevitably slows reflexes and thought processes. Just as a man of 80 may walk more slowly than he did in his youth and may not be able to catch a ball thrown at him suddenly, he probably will think more slowly than he did in his prime. However, one psychologist, Jack Botwinick, head of Washington University's Aging and Development Program in St. Louis, thinks the effect may be counteracted by life habits of exercise.

Learning also depends on response speed, and several studies have

shown that, while you can teach an old dog new tricks, it takes longer. Older persons can learn as well as younger ones if the teaching process is slowed to match their pace, and if the information is delivered with more clarity and emphasis (louder sounds, brighter images).

Over a wide range of mental activities, however, speed of response is irrelevant and intelligence survives intact. Old people who are in good health do not lose their judgment, their ability to think abstractly or their knowledge. Vocabulary, number skills, inductive reasoning and all the harvest of education and experience function until very near the end; some abilities, particularly verbal skills, may even increase with age. These are the components of intelligence that have come to be respected as wisdom. In relatively stable and unchanging societies this wisdom has been almost synonymous with age and has made advanced years a prerequisite for leadership. The more volatile cultures of the industrialized world may place a premium on youth, yet even they value the talents that seem to build over the decades, and they, too, give political control to older citizens. Many chiefs of government are over 60 years old, and in recent decades power has been wielded effectively by such septuagenarians as Golda Meir and Chou En-lai.

Few people fail to recognize the physical and mental changes, for good or ill, that overtake them with passing time. The bag of groceries from the market is heavier than it used to be; younger persons catch on to some things faster, yet cannot so easily grasp the full significance of what they have experienced. Such consequences of age are generally so obvious that a psychological shifting of gears is necessary. A reassessment of personality is called for. Once again the essential human questions must be faced: Who am I? What is expected of me? What do I expect of myself? How should I act?

According to Robert Butler, a psychiatrist and gerontologist, an old person is redefining his identity when he reminisces about events everyone else has forgotten or spends hours looking through old photographs. Butler concluded that this is an important adaptive process of later life and should not be dismissed as idle "dwelling in the past." He called it the life review and described it as a serious attempt by the individual to sift through his life for nuggets of meaning, to resolve old doubts and conflicts that could never before be surveyed, and to reexamine and restructure his identity in light of past and present experience.

One reason an old person may find it necessary to reexamine his past and shift his behavioral strategies is that his identity and independence are under attack by a number of internal and external forces. He finds fewer options open to him and feels set aside. "As the limits of self-determination grow narrower," one British octogenarian observed, "the aging person clings more anxiously to what remains." Repeated rejection undermines the old person's sense of usefulness, a vital ingredient of the healthy ego. If he is unneeded he feels he has no value, and hence is nothing. To avoid making mistakes that will bring ridicule from the young, he becomes more cautious, and temporizes in his decision making. Trial and error are not for him; he will think things through before acting, and if he is not sure what to do he will do nothing.

Such psychological changes have been analyzed in detail by the Kansas City Study of Adult Life, a long-term investigation of aging carried out by a group at the University of Chicago that included gerontologist Bernice Neugarten. The researchers found that as people age they regard themselves as more passive and conformist; they become more preoccupied with their own inner concerns and needs; they make fewer emotional commitments to, and become less interested in, the outer world. According to Neugarten, "Older men and women, in verbalizing opinions in dogmatic terms, in failing to clarify . . . relationships, and in using eccentric methods of communication, gave evidence of lessened sensitivity to the reactions of others." It was not that they could not make themselves clearer, Neugarten felt; they simply did not care. Rather than weakness or insensitivity, this attitude may simply reflect a freedom that comes only with age—freedom from obligations, from the need to respond as expected.

But while old people turn inward and care less about others' opinions of them, they do not necessarily want to withdraw from society. The Kansas City researchers found that most aging people gradually cut down the amount of time they spend with other people and the amount of effort they put into their various social roles, but the disengagement seems primarily a response. Society withdraws first, forcing the older people to do the same. Even while they are focusing more on themselves, the elderly regret the loosening of social ties. As Neugarten and her colleagues reported, "There appear to be two sets of values operating simultaneously. . . . On the one hand, the desire to stay active in order to maintain a sense of self-worth; on the other hand, the desire to withdraw from social commitments and to pursue a more leisurely and a more contemplative way of life."

Analyzing such reactions, Neugarten and her associates classified individuals according to their ability to adapt themselves to old age. The classification includes eight different adapting patterns among four types of personalities.

The most successful adjustments were made by the integrated personalities—the mature and flexible people with rich inner lives—who were open to new stimuli and not afraid of their emotions. All of them were happy but some of them were involved in social activities and some were not.

One group of integrated elderly comprised the reorganizers, those "who substitute new activities for lost ones; who, when they retire from work, give time to community affairs or to church or to other associations. They reorganize their patterns of activity."

A second group of integrated personalities, the "focused," achieved satisfaction by selecting one or two areas of activity. One retired man was "preoccupied with the roles of homemaker, parent and husband. He had withdrawn from work and from club memberships and welcomed the opportunity to live a happy and full life with his family."

A third group of integrated persons, the "disengaged," abandoned their commitments, and were content to do so. They were "self-directed persons, not shallow, with an interest in the world but an interest that is not imbedded in a network of social interactions. . . . They have chosen what might be called a 'rocking-chair' approach to old age."

Two quite different patterns were seen among the "armored," or "defended," personalities—striving, ambitious people who keep a tight control over their anxieties and impulses. To some among them, aging was a threat and satisfaction was found by holding on to the patterns of their middle age. Others deliberately constricted their social interactions and closed themselves off against experience. Since they regarded this strategy as a successful response to old age, they were moderately satisfied with their low levels of activity.

Less successful styles of aging were found in "passive-dependent" personalities. The "succorance-seeking" got along with medium activity and medium satisfaction as long as they had someone to lean on. Below them in the scales of satisfaction were the "apathetic," whose "long-standing patterns of passivity and apathy" prevented them from doing anything—like the man who let his wife answer the interviewers' questions for him.

Finally, at the bottom of the scale, the investigators noted the "unintegrated" personalities with a disorganized pattern of aging. Low both in activity and satisfaction, they could neither control their emotions nor think clearly.

Neugarten and her colleagues came to the conclusion that all of these people were merely repeating the patterns of a lifetime. They did not accept the view that personality changes markedly after its fundamental

Good cheer in a home for the aged

It has been three centuries since the English invented the institution that evolved into the modern nursing home for the aged. Today, a whole spectrum of such homes—financed by government support, philanthropy or patients' fees—exists around the world; even in Britain and the Soviet Union, which provide homes subsidized by the government, private facilities are available for those who can afford to pay for their services. In the United States, public and private homes are long established, but the best care, according to many experts, is generally offered by those that are run by religious groups.

Such a home is New York City's 509-bed Daughters of Jacob Nursing Home, where patients lead lives as productively active as possible. New arrivals are urged to enter whatever work, discussion group or recreation program suits them: women may get together to bake pastry for the holidays or to attend dance classes. Many patients, finding themselves again involved in meaningful activities, experience a rebirth of their independence.

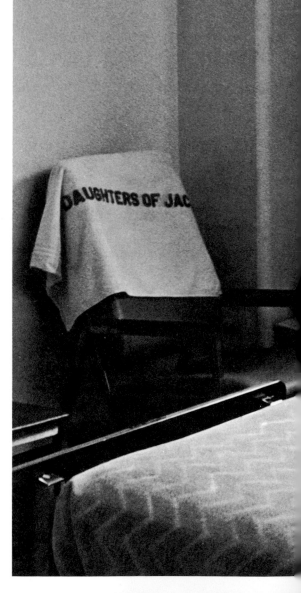

Keeping up with the world, members of the current-events program listen as a volunteer reads a newspaper article, which they will then debate. The current-events group regularly draws from 10 to 60 people, for sometimes heated discussions of everything from the state of the economy to foreign affairs.

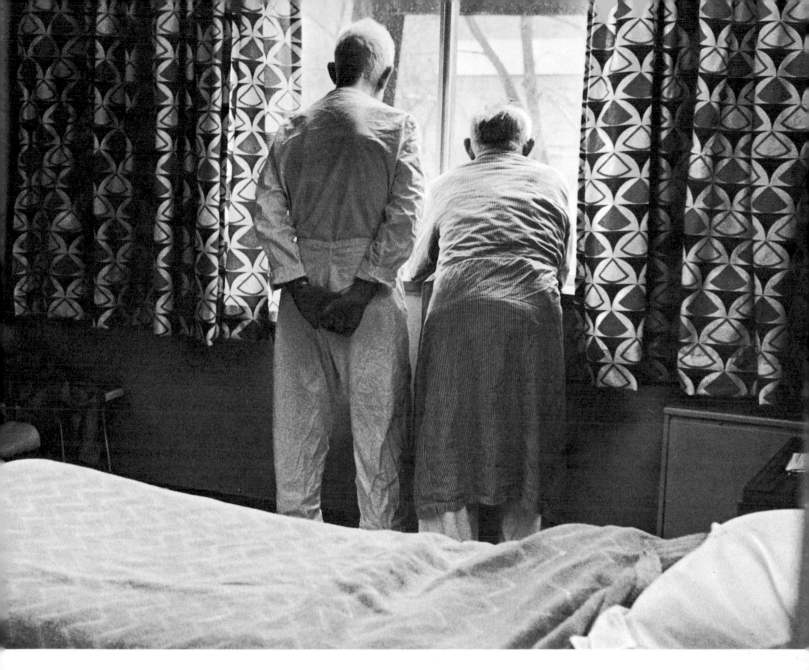

Roommates in the skilled nursing facility
—that section of the home reserved for
patients requiring extensive care—engage
in a quiet chat. For many patients who
lived alone before coming to the
home, loneliness is alleviated by the
attachments they develop for roommates.

Serving as a waiter, William Tauber, 86,
carries a tray full of cake to fellow
patients in the dining room. He is one of
a small group of resident volunteers who
help the staff care for the more infirm
patients, in a program intended to restore
the volunteer's sense of usefulness.

147

form is fixed in childhood, and maintained that its original outlines can only be refined, not restructured. "In normal men and women there is no sharp discontinuity of personality with age, but instead an increasing consistency. Those characteristics that have been central to the personality seem to become even more clearly delineated, and those values the individual has been cherishing become even more salient."

These patterns of change depend upon reasonably good health. Sooner or later, the old person's capacity to enjoy himself and to adapt to his changing circumstances may be impaired by physical deterioration. Eventually, complete independence to continue a personal life style becomes impossible. The aged person who is no longer physically capable of caring for himself must have help. How that help is to be provided has become one of the major problems facing modern society. It is a new problem simply because of numbers; in the past, elders were so few and survived such a short time after becoming inactive that their care never was a burden—their children and grandchildren looked after them for the brief period between enfeeblement and death. Today, not only do more people live to become old, but they can be kept comfortable, mentally alert and a miraculous joy to their families for decades after they have lost the physical ability to care completely for themselves. Mingled with the love and warmth their families feel in their presence is a responsibility. By the year 2000, according to one estimate, 121 million workers in the United States will be supporting 83 million retired people (and 97 million children). Already the impact of this new balance of population is being felt. One woman devoted 14 years to ministering first to her father-in-law and then to her mother-in-law, and had to take care of her father after that.

In some modern societies responsibility for the infirm elderly is still accepted as a matter of course—and enjoyed—by the old person's family. Oriental households, including those of industrialized Japan and China, continue to give old people the place of honor and to tend privately to their every need, right up to the final one of preparation for burial. In many countries of Europe, on the other hand, the state has taken over, providing a spectrum of services to tend to the elderly in their own homes or in institutions—regardless of attentions the family provides. The United States is in the midst of a painful transition. The inability of families to care completely for their own aged members has been recognized, but the programs of assistance so far developed have not proved entirely satisfactory. Financial aid is cumbersome and often inequitably distributed. Schemes for providing personalized help at home are still experimental. And a massive, costly attempt to offer institutional care in nursing homes has been disappointing.

One in five older Americans spends his declining years in a nursing home, and the figure has been steadily rising since the adoption of the Medicare program in 1965, which made federal funds available for the care of the elderly in licensed institutions but provided little or nothing for care at home. Most elderly people try to avoid these institutions, since they are by necessity impersonal and often deprive the patients of favorite foods, activities and opportunities for social stimulation. Psychiatrists and specialists in the care of the elderly have criticized the institutions because they generally take away more of the individual's independence than he is ready to relinquish. "Even a normal person would deteriorate in a nursing home," said Robert Kahn, a University of Chicago psychiatrist. Indeed, a study of old women in one of the most highly regarded of these institutions, the Home for Aged and Infirm Hebrews of New York, showed that those women who lived in a custodial nursing-home wing feared death more than those of similar age and health who were quartered in their own apartments within the home.

This represents the gloomy side of the picture, however. Thousands of old people enjoy long years of life in nursing homes. Some are there because they have no families, because their children cannot afford to take them in, or because all the adults in their families work all day so there is no one at home to see that Grandpa gets his lunch. But many others, who could live alone or with their families, prefer the security of professional care and the sociability of being among people their own age away from the noise and bustle of young households.

The nursing home is obviously not a solution, however, for those who like to live on their own—as the great majority of Americans do—and could manage well if they were given assistance with cleaning, marketing, cooking and errands. Experiments aimed at providing such help have been conducted in a number of cities, particularly in the Middle West, where there are both a large population of the elderly and a strong tradition of independence.

In Kansas, where by the 1970s 12 per cent of the population was over 65 (one of the highest proportions in the United States) and 87 per cent of the elderly lived in their own houses or apartments, the city of Lawrence was one community helping old people to carry on at home. The services included a minibus transportation system that took anyone over 60 anywhere he wanted to go within the city limits, a clinic to give regular tests and nutritional advice, a handyman program to make inexpensive home repairs, and a network of cafeterias serving hot lunches.

In addition, a Meals on Wheels service made the rounds once a day to people who were housebound. For recreation, there were card games, bingo and weekend excursions to museums, sports events and festivals. An information center provided advice on financial aid.

One spry old lady—who rode the minibus as often as 10 times a week, ate at a luncheon cafeteria every day, served as a volunteer for meal preparation, patronized the health clinic regularly, and enjoyed the weekend trips—said, "I just hope they don't cut off the money for it." Her enthusiasm was echoed by David Crowley, executive director of the Ohio Commission on Aging, who estimated that 25 per cent of nursing home patients across the state could live in their own homes if more such assistance were available. Crowley told of the value of one geriatric program to a 72-year-old Cleveland woman whose husband had had a stroke. With the help of a volunteer who shopped and cleaned house for the couple and made sure they had a hot meal each day, the wife was able to handle the difficult task of caring for her bedridden husband at home. "They are examples of two people who can make it with a little help on the side," said Crowley. "If you separated them I don't think either would live too long."

Such broad, personal assistance to the elderly is routine in Sweden, where the state assumes full responsibility for the welfare of the aged, and makes it easy for them to get along on their own. The vast majority of elderly people live in their own homes supported by generous government pensions and assisted by Home Samaritans, who visit regularly to clean, shop and cook at little or no cost to the pensioner. A grown daughter who takes over this role for her aged parent can be paid for it, just as a stranger would, and since this money comes from the high taxes Swedes pay, they see nothing unnatural in taking it. What does seem unnatural, because it is never necessary, is installing an aged parent in one's home. That is virtually unheard of except in rural areas.

Swedish elderly who prefer not to live in their own apartments can get an inexpensive private room in a well-equipped, professionally staffed old-age home, or move to one of the government service hotels for old people, where food and help are available. The incapacitated are tended to in nursing homes. Hospital stays are free, doctors and drugs are cheap, government-run leisure centers offer lectures, study courses and cut-price junkets, and the aged can get out and around as much as they like on their half-price bus and rail passes—they are even provided six free taxi trips a month. The Swedish system frees the elderly of financial worries, guards their health, encourages their independence and respects their intelligence—and thereby allows them

continued on page 154

Caucasus elder Q. Jonushian, claiming 110 years, ruefully says, "I lost my virility at 98."

"Centenarians" of the Caucasus

For decades villagers in the Caucasus Mountains of the southwestern U.S.S.R. have been touted for longevity. Thousands of the region's citizens claim to be over 100; hundreds say they will never see 120 again. A television film of the Caucasus villagers, shown in the United States, featured a robust old man in his nineties busily chopping wood. The old man normally worked a full day, the commentator said, but on this occasion he was taking half a day off—to attend a birthday party for his mother, 141. The old woman herself appeared and danced a jig.

Western scientists have long been skeptical of such claims, because they come largely from areas lacking precise age records. But the Caucasus centenarians were not unmasked until Zhores A. Medvedev, a famed Soviet biologist, got into political trouble and opted for exile in London. From his refuge he blew the whistle.

Not only are birth certificates notably lacking in the Caucasus, he revealed, but the records that exist are often altered to increase male ages to help men evade the draft. Medvedev explained that the cult of old people was fostered by Joseph Stalin, a native of the Caucasus, and the ages of its natives were exaggerated to please him.

Meanwhile, the oldtimers continue claiming extraordinary ages for themselves and—as seen on the following pages—offering some highly contradictory formulas for their longevity.

Khfaf Lasuria, allegedly 141, says, "I sip vodka at breakfast."

"I never read books or worry," says M. Surmeneliani, reportedly 108.

"Keep an interest in ladies," advises G. Chapnian, said to be 117.

"I don't smoke, I like wine," says T. Gunba, who settles for a paltry 98.

"If I get any closer, I'll kiss her," says A. Butba, who claims 120 and ascribes his liveliness to his youthful wife Marusia, a mere 109.

to grow old in full possession of their identity. Not surprisingly, perhaps, the life expectancy of the Swedes (73.3) is among the highest in the world. The monetary cost is high: a Swede who earns $6,000 a year pays a third of his income in taxes that help support welfare programs for the aged. For higher income brackets the tax bite is even larger.

Exactly the opposite system is in effect in Japan. The government and private employers pay pensions to the elderly, and the cost of medical care is minimal, but otherwise the state does not interfere. In Japan, a feudalistic, agrarian ethic survives in a modern setting, and 75 per cent of all people over the age of 65 live with their children. In many cases it is their *children* who live with *them,* for the oldest son may never have moved away from home. Instead, when he married, he brought his bride into his parents' household and settled in to carry on the family line. Even if the children have moved away, one or another will take the old people in without hesitation when the time comes. The Japanese consider it their natural duty to care for and support an ill or feeble parent; throughout the Orient, to neglect a parent or to leave a parent in the care of strangers is to disgrace the family name.

Japanese old people still enjoy much of the respect and status that their hierarchical society traditions and Confucian philosophy have always granted them. They remain productive, helping with housework, child care, gardening and, in some cases, the family business; they join associations and participate in community life; they are awarded government medals for attaining certain ages; and they always receive the seat of honor, the deepest bows, the best clothes and the first dip in the family tub (although males always precede females to the bath). They may no longer wield absolute authority over their children but they are consulted regularly on family decisions. Respect for seniority is so ingrained that when older persons are addressed even the language shifts gears and a special set of pronouns and suffixes is required.

Nowhere in the Japanese style of growing old is there any demand for self-determination, or any fear of dependence on family. The Chinese also welcome dependency in old age, for they regard individualism as merely pride. And they revere old age because, as the Chinese philosopher Lin Yutang wrote a few decades ago, "How can one be thought wise unless one is thought to be old? And what do the young really know about life, about marriage, and about the true values?"

"The fact that the old men of America still insist on being so busy and active can be directly traced to individualism carried to a foolish extent," Lin wrote in an essay "On Growing Old Gracefully." "Can one not forget the individual and his pride of self in a general scheme of

The contented oldsters in the crowd shown here are, from an actuarial standpoint, among the most fortunate people in the world. They live in England, where the life expectancy—72.3 years—is one of the highest on earth.

The international longevity gap

A baby born in Japan can expect to live twice as long as one born in Bangladesh. He can also expect to outlive a Nigerian by 32.3 years and an Indonesian by 25.8. Such startling discrepancies in life expectancy between industrialized and nonindustrialized countries, from United Nations figures for the world's 14 most densely populated countries, result from better medical care in richer lands, which has enabled more young people to survive to grow old.

But the life-expectancy gap is steadily narrowing. In the United States, life expectancy at birth increased only 1.4 years in a 14-year period; in Brazil it went up 8.8 years in two decades. The effect on world population has been dramatic: in 1970 there were nearly 300 million people over 60, an increase of 100 per cent during 30 years.

LIFE EXPECTANCY AT BIRTH FOR THE WORLD'S 14 MOST POPULATED NATIONS

JAPAN	73.3
FRANCE	72.6
UNITED KINGDOM	72.3
ITALY	72.0
UNITED STATES	71.3
WEST GERMANY	70.6
UNION OF SOVIET SOCIALIST REPUBLICS	70.4
CHINA (MAINLAND)	61.6
BRAZIL	61.4
PAKISTAN	49.8
INDIA	49.5
INDONESIA	47.5
NIGERIA	41.0
BANGLADESH	35.8

home life in which men are justly taken care of by their parents and, having in turn taken care of their children, are also justly taken care of by the latter? The Chinese have not got the sense of individual independence because the whole conception of life is based upon mutual help within the home; hence there is no shame attached to the circumstance of one's being served by his children in the sunset of one's life. Rather it is considered good luck to have children who can take care of one. . . . The symphony of life should end with a grand finale of peace and serenity and material comfort and spiritual contentment, and not with the crash of a broken drum or cracked cymbals."

The end of the symphony can be approached with serenity and contentment by those elderly who are capable of seeing themselves as a part of an inexorable process. Like the Chinese elder who is reminded by the attention of dutiful children that the family will live on, they simply learn to accept death.

Old people generally show less anxiety about death than younger ones. But the concept still is hard for most individuals in the Western world to accept. For, as Robert Butler pointed out, "One must be alive, in control and aware of what is happening. The greater and more self-centered or narcissistic Western emphasis on individuality and control makes death an outrage, a tremendous affront to man, rather than the logical and necessary process of old life making way for new." When a Westerner says, "Life is cheap in the Orient," he may be reflecting the fact that the East has learned to accept death with more equanimity.

The difference between the contrasting attitudes was starkly revealed to an American married to a Japanese and living in Japan. Like most American children he had been shielded from death as a boy. He remembered "not even being told of the death of my invalid grandmother, who died while I was away for the summer. When I came back I was expected to infer from significant silences and facial expressions that she had died." Years later in Japan he was dismayed to learn that his children were expected to participate in the ritual of preparing their maternal grandfather for burial. "To me it was barbaric to confront children with death that way," he relates, "and I nearly forbade my kids to join their cousins around the body. At the last minute I did let them perform this final, kind duty for a beloved grandfather. I'm glad I did; the experience was much more traumatic for me than for them."

It may be the fear of one's own death that causes people to abhor and avoid the death of others. Some philosophers believe that it is good to fear death, that human beings were given the knowledge of mortality precisely in order that they might fear it and, in fearing nothingness,

Expectancy: the female's lead

Everyone knows that women generally live longer than men, but the overall difference is much less than most people think. The figures usually quoted are those for life expectancy at birth, which exaggerate the female advantage because young girls are less vulnerable than boys to disease and accident. But as life expectancy changes with age, the relative handicap of being male decreases. The United States figures below, similar to those in all affluent countries, indicate that a man who makes it to the age of 80 can expect to reach 86.4; his wife can look ahead to just a bit more, 87.9.

	LIFE EXPECTANCY	
	MALE	FEMALE
at birth	67.6	75.3
at 10	69.3	76.8
at 20	69.9	77.1
at 30	70.9	77.5
at 40	71.8	78.0
at 50	73.4	79.1
at 60	76.2	80.9
at 70	80.4	83.6
at 80	86.4	87.9

strive to leave some trace of their existence and thus build civilization. But to others, the weakening of religious belief in an afterlife has produced "a frightening void."

Even medical professionals who see death constantly are afraid of it. In fact, one psychological study of doctors indicated that they have a greater fear of death than most people and may have become doctors in order to fight that fear. Anxiety over death was exacerbated in the days when most people died before aging, before they had a chance to make a mark or to savor life, and consequently death *was* a tragedy. As recently as 1900, only 15 per cent of the deaths in the United States were deaths of people over 65, but by the mid-1970s more than 70 per cent of those dying had reached that age of greater acceptance.

As more and more people survive to old age, there are signs of a more open, more natural attitude toward death, an attitude that recognizes death as an inevitable part of the life cycle. Yet acceptance of death is still difficult to achieve. Chicago psychiatrist Elisabeth Kübler-Ross observed five stages of awareness of approaching death. First comes denial, "This can't be happening to me." This stage, during which the dying person seeks frantically for new diagnoses and cures, can be good for those people who were always fighters—even if they do not win the battle and prolong their lives, they gain satisfaction from the struggle. Then comes anger—at God, doctors, family, friends. This, said Kübler-Ross, should be tolerated and not taken personally, for the dying person is merely reacting against the health of others. Bargaining is next, during which the patient seeks a little more time for good behavior or for prayers to God. In this stage many people are able to hang on to life until after a birthday or a significant holiday. (The Jewish death rate seems to dip in the weeks before Yom Kippur, the Day of Atonement). In the depression stage the individual may cry and grieve and refuse to see his family, not because he no longer cares about them but because he must begin to disassociate himself from loved ones he knows he will soon have to leave behind.

Not until the dying person has finished mourning, finished his anger and envy, will he achieve acceptance and "contemplate his coming end with a certain degree of quiet expectation." The stage is almost clear of emotion, said Kübler-Ross, and acceptance is expressed mostly in silence. "He may just hold our hand and . . . we may together listen to the song of a bird from the outside." No words are needed, no television, few visitors. For someone at peace with himself, death is, wrote Erik Erikson, "the acceptance of one's one and only life cycle as something that had to be and that, by necessity, permitted of no substitutions."

Proud death of a family man

Seeing his grandson Dan at work readying the garden for spring planting, Gramp anxiously asks, "Do you think this guy will mind us plowing up his land?" as Mark takes his picture. Told that it was his own land, Gramp laughed, and so did the boys. But it was the first time Mark and Dan had seen the disorientation that was overtaking their grandfather.

PHOTOGRAPHED BY
MARK AND DAN JURY

Throughout his long life, Frank Tugend was a devoted family man. When he was 11, he went to work in the coal mines near his home in Scranton, Pennsylvania, to help support his brothers and sisters. After he had labored there 21 years, he invested all his savings in a piece of land in the country and began to build a house there with his own hands, working on it whenever he had free time. It was, he said, to be his family's "estate," and over the years it became the focal point of life for four generations of Tugends. In it Frank and his wife raised their brood, and to it their grandchildren came each summer, ultimately bringing their own sons and daughters as well.

The years passed, and Gramp, as the family now called him, gradually began to fail. The first disturbing sign appeared when a friend found him downtown one day, sitting in the car, not knowing who he was or how to get home. The friend showed him the way back to the house, and Gramp drove home, parked his car in the garage and never used it again.

A doctor explained Gramp's befuddlement: at the age of 78, he was suffering from senility. There was no treatment for his condition, and the symptoms of forgetfulness and disorientation could only grow worse.

The doctor told the family that they could put Gramp into a nursing home, but they knew he would not want it that way. And so, as recorded in pictures taken by two of his grandsons, Dan and Mark Jury, who are professional photographers, Gramp's family comforted him and cared for him, enabling a proud old man to die in his own house in his own way.

*Continuing an old custom that Gramp
loved, four generations of the family sit
down to a picnic dinner at the edge
of the woods near their country home.
Because Gramp so enjoyed family
festivities such as birthday parties, his
children and grandchildren often
staged them, even when no one actually
had a birthday to be celebrated.*

Still alert and hearty, Gramp indulges his photographer grandsons by sitting for a portrait alongside a lake he liked to fish. Gramp had always been anxious that his children and grandchildren learn to enjoy the outdoors, and years earlier he had turned the creek on his land into a community swimming hole and built the youngsters a rowboat in which to cruise its waters.

As Gramp's mind grew more disordered, the bond with great-granddaughter Hillary became especially strong. He would regale her with descriptions of imaginary creatures—red rabbits in the refrigerator, a tiger-headed animal on the lawn. Sometimes she and Gramp would run out of a room, chortling with glee at their escape from the beasts.

Returning from a walk he had taken over his land to find some fresh flowers for his wife, Nan, Gramp offers her a bouquet, not realizing that it consists of weeds. Sadly touched and anxious to please him, Nan thanks him warmly as she reaches out to take his present.

Dan spruces up Gramp with a haircut and a shave in a ritual whose meaning gradually changed. When Gramp first lost the ability to shave, he would get upset as his beard grew, and would ask one of the boys to shave him. Later, he would sometimes balk until, as Dan recalls, "I would say, 'Well, Gramp, you'll make a fine-looking hippie.' And Gramp would dash for the nearest chair to get shaved."

Basking in the fading autumn sun, Nan
Tugend turns a gaze full of loving
concern toward her husband of 57 years.
Of all the family, it was she who tried
most to puzzle out what experiences
Gramp underwent as he withdrew into his
own world. When he stared silently out
the window for hours on end, she would
sit by him, wondering, and asking
the others, "What can he be thinking?"

One day, Gramp removed his false teeth
and announced that he was no longer
going to eat. By now his physical
condition had seriously deteriorated, and
he committed himself to face the end
with determination. The family agonized
over their responsibility—he could have
been hospitalized for intravenous
feeding but they decided against it. "The
thought of this independent man strapped
to a bed with tubes protruding from
his arms was repugnant to us," says Mark.

167

Gramp's widow, Nan (second from left), is comforted by friends and relatives as she leaves the cemetery following his funeral. He died at age 81 exactly three weeks after he started to fast, succeeding in his determination to die on his own terms. His family's grief was tempered with awe, Mark remembers. "We felt an enormous amount of respect for this tough old coal miner. Looking at his empty bed, I thought, 'You pulled it off, Gramp. You really pulled it off.'"

Bibliography

Books

Beals, Ralph L., and Harry Hoijer, *An Introduction to Anthropology*. The Macmillan Co., 1971.

Bergler, Edmund, *The Revolt of the Middle-aged Man*. A. A. Wyn, 1954.

Blaine, Graham B., Jr., *Patience and Fortitude, The Parents' Guide to Adolescence*. Little, Brown & Co., 1962.

Botwinick, Jack, *Aging and Behavior*. Springer Publishing Co., 1973.

Boyd, Rosamonde Ramsay, and Charles G. Oakes, *Foundations of Practical Gerontology*. University of South Carolina Press, 1969.

Buechler, Hans, and Judith-Maria, *The Bolivian Aymara*. Holt, Rinehart and Winston, 1971.

Butler, Robert N., *Why Survive? Being Old in America*. Harper & Row, Publishers, 1975.

Campbell, J. K., *Honour, Family and Patronage: A Study of Institutions and Moral Values in a Greek Mountain Community*. Clarendon Press, 1964.

Clark, Margaret, and Barbara Gallatin Anderson, *Culture and Aging*. Charles C Thomas, 1967.

Deutsch, Helene, *Motherhood*. The Psychology of Women, Vol. 2. Grune & Stratton, 1945.

Eisdorfer, Carl, and M. Powell Lawton, eds., *The Psychology of Adult Development and Aging*. American Psychological Association, 1973.

Erikson, Erik H.:
Childhood and Society. W. W. Norton & Co., 1963.
Identity: Youth and Crisis. W. W. Norton & Co., 1968.
Insight and Responsibility. W. W. Norton & Co., 1964.

Evans, Richard I., *Dialogue with Erik Erikson*. Harper & Row, Publishers, 1967.

Fakhouri, Hani, *Kafr El-Elow, An Egyptian Village in Transition*. Holt, Rinehart and Winston, 1972.

Freud, Anna, *The Ego and the Mechanisms of Defense*. International Universities Press, 1946.

Friedl, Ernestine, *Vasilika, A Village in Modern Greece*. Holt, Rinehart and Winston, 1962.

Ginott, Haim G., *Between Parent & Teenager*. Avon Books, 1969.

Ginzberg, Eli, et al., *Occupational Choice*. Columbia University Press, 1966.

Gottlieb, David, Jon Reeves and Warren D. TenHouten, *The Emergence of Youth Societies: A Cross-Cultural Approach*. The Free Press, 1966.

Goulet, L. R., and Paul B. Baltes, eds., *Research and Theory*. Life-Span Developmental Psychology. Academic Press, 1970.

Hendin, David, *Death as a Fact of Life*. W. W. Norton & Co., 1973.

Jaques, Elliott, *Work, Creativity & Social Justice*. Heinemann, 1970.

Kagan, Jerome, and Robert Coles, eds., *12 to 16, Early Adolescence*. W. W. Norton & Co., 1972.

Kastenbaum, Robert, and Ruth Aisenberg, *The Psychology of Death*. Springer Publishing Co., 1972.

Keniston, Kenneth:
Young Radicals. Harcourt, Brace & World, 1968.
The Uncommitted. Dell Publishing Co., 1965.

Kübler-Ross, Elisabeth, *On Death and Dying*. The Macmillan Co., 1973.

Lasswell, Marcia E. and Thomas E., eds., *Love, Marriage, Family*. Scott, Foresman and Company, 1973.

LeShan, Eda J., *The Wonderful Crisis of Middle Age*. David McKay Co., 1973.

Lidz, Theodore, *The Person*. Basic Books, 1968.

Mace, David and Vera, *Marriage: East & West*, Doubleday & Co., 1959.

Masters, William H., and Virginia E. Johnson, *Human Sexual Response*. Little, Brown & Co., 1966.

Mead, Margaret, *Coming of Age in Samoa*. Random House, 1953.

Musgrove, Frank, *Youth and the Social Order*. Indiana University Press, 1964.

Neugarten, Bernice L., ed., *Middle Age and Aging: A Reader in Social Psychology*. University of Chicago Press, 1968.

Nomads of the World, National Geographic Society, 1971.

Normal Adolescence: Its Dynamics and Impact, formulated by the Committee on Adolescence, Group for the Advancement of Psychiatry. Charles Scribner's Sons, 1968.

Rapoport, Robert N., *Mid-Career Development*. Tavistock Publications, 1970.

Ravich, Robert A., and Barbara Wyden, *Predictable Pairing*. Peter H. Wyden, 1974.

Ricks, D. F., A. Thomas and M. Roff, eds., *Life History Research in Psychopathology*. Vol. 3. University of Minnesota Press, 1974.

Riley, Matilda White, Marilyn Johnson and Ann Foner, *Aging and Society*. Russell Sage Foundation, 1972.

Sears, Robert R., and S. Shirley Feldman, eds., *The Seven Ages of Man*. William Kaufmann, 1973.

Stone, L. Joseph, and Joseph Church, *Childhood and Adolescence*. Random House, 1973.

Streib, Gordon F., and Clement J. Schneider, *Retirement in American Society*. Cornell University Press, 1971.

Tanner, J. M., *Growth at Adolescence*. Blackwell Scientific Publications, Oxford University Press, 1962.

Wilson, Monica, *Good Company*. Oxford University Press, 1951.

Youth, Transition to Adulthood. Report of the Panel on Youth of the President's Science Advisory Committee. University of Chicago Press, 1974.

Periodicals

Butler, Robert N., "Successful Aging and the Role of the Life Review." *Journal of the American Geriatrics Society*, Vol. XXII, No. 12 (December 1974), pp. 529-535.

Greenfeld, Josh, "A Dramatic Sense of Age . . . A Sudden Sniff of Death." *Today's Health* (March 1973), pp. 44-48.

Hayflick, Leonard, "Human Cells and Aging." *Scientific American* (March 1968), Vol. 218, No. 3, pp. 32-37.

Leaf, Alexander, "Every Day Is a Gift When You Are over 100." *National Geographic* (January 1973).

Neugarten, Bernice L., "A New Look at Menopause," in *The Female Experience* published by *Psychology Today*, 1973, pp. 39ff.

Neugarten, Bernice L., Vivian Wood, Ruth J. Kraines and Barbara Loomis, "Women's Attitudes toward the Menopause." *Vita Humana*, Vol. 6 (1963), pp. 140-151.

Sherman, Susan R., "Satisfaction with Retirement Housing: Attitudes, Recommendations and Moves." *Aging and Human Development*, Vol. 3, No. 4 (1972).

Vaillant, George E., and Charles C. MacArthur, "Natural History of Male Psychologic Health: I. The Adult Life Cycle from 18-50." *Seminars in Psychiatry*, Vol. 4, No. 4 (November 1972).

Picture Credits

The sources for the illustrations in this book are shown below. Credits for illustrations from left to right are separated by semicolons; from top to bottom they are separated by dashes.

Cover—Ken Kay. 6—James Carroll. 11 —Figures courtesy of the United Nations Population Division, New York City —Gina Lollobrigida. 14—Victor Englebert. 16—Dmitri Kessel from TIME-LIFE Picture Agency; Ted Streshinsky from TIME-LIFE Picture Agency. 17—Jim Collison from TIME-LIFE Picture Agency; courtesy Yale University; Mottke Weissman. 20, 21—Courtesy André Grabowicz. 23—Staatliche Museen Preussischer Kulturbesitz Gemäldegalerie, Berlin West. 28, 29—Hassoldt Davis from Rapho/Photo Researchers. 30, 31—Ken Heyman; Ted Spiegel from Black Star—Zelas/Duttilleaux from Woodfin Camp and Associates. 32—D. Jacobson from Editorial Photocolor Archives—Bruce Roberts from Rapho/Photo Researchers. 33—Mirella Ricciardi. 34, 35—Neal Slavin. 36, 37—Hans Hoefer from Woodfin Camp and Associates; Horst Munzig. 38 —Charles Gatewood. 41—Reprinted from *Psychology Today* magazine, February 1975. Copyright © 1974 Ziff Davis Publishing Co. All rights reserved. 43—John Bryson from TIME-LIFE Picture Agency. 44, 45—Bruce Davidson from Magnum. 47 —Roger Malloch from Magnum. 51 —Alex Webb. 52, 53—Alex Webb except top left Alex Webb from Magnum. 54 —Alex Webb. 56—Henri Cartier-Bresson from Magnum. 58—Robert Burroughs. 60, 61—Ira Rosenberg for *Detroit Free Press.* 62—Ken Heyman. 64—David Maybury-Lewis from Anthro-Photo. 66—Mary Ellen Mark. 69—Reprinted from *Psychology Today* magazine, February 1975. Copyright © 1974 Ziff Davis Publishing Co. All rights reserved. 72—Ken Heyman. 73—E. J. Bottomley, Syndication International. 76, 77—Victor Englebert. 81 —Marilyn Silverstone from Magnum. 84 —Grey Villet from TIME-LIFE Picture Agency. 86—Max Scheler, Stern. 88 through 99—Courtesy Gerd Pless Agency, Munich. 88 through 91—Elizabeth Pfefferkorn. 92 through 95—Will McBride. 96, 97—Will McBride; Elizabeth Pfefferkorn. 98, 99—Elizabeth Pfefferkorn. 100—Mary Ellen Mark. 103—Reprinted from *Psychology Today* magazine, February 1975. Copyright © 1974 Ziff Davis Publishing Co. All rights reserved. 104—Elliott Erwitt from Magnum © 1969. 107—Drawing based on a study by International Health Foundation, Geneva, Switzerland. 108—Morris Berman for *Pittsburgh Post-Gazette.* 113—Inge Morath from Magnum. 115—Jean Luce-Hure for *The New York Times*; Carlo Bavagnoli from TIME-LIFE Picture Agency —Mark Kauffman from TIME-LIFE Picture Agency; David Lees. 116—Jean Luce-Hure for *The New York Times* —Carlo Bavagnoli from TIME-LIFE Picture Agency. 117—Mark Kauffman from TIME-LIFE Picture Agency. 118— David Lees. 120—Robert Burroughs. 122 through 131—Bill Ray from TIME-LIFE Picture Agency. 132—Thomas Höpker from Woodfin Camp and Associates. 136—© copyright 1974 by Mark Jury. 138—Rudy Vetter for Action/FGP. 139—Paul Conklin for Action/Score—Susan Biddle for Action/RSVP. 142—Constantine Manos from Magnum. 146, 147 —Sepp Seitz from Magnum. 151, 152, 153 —John Launois from Black Star. 155 —Marc Riboud from Magnum—Figures courtesy United Nations Population Division, New York City. 157—Figures courtesy of Department of Health, Education and Welfare. 158 through 169—© copyright 1975 by Mark and Dan Jury.

Acknowledgments

The author and editors of this book wish to thank the following persons and institutions: Ella Drucker, New York City; Leroy E. Duncan Jr., M.D., Chief, Adult Development and Aging Branch, National Institute of Child Health and Human Development, Bethesda, Maryland; Franco Ferrarotti, Director, Institute of Sociology, Rome University, Italy; Professor Michael Fogarty, The Center for Studies in Social Policy, London, England; Dr. Roger Gould, Associate Professor of Psychiatry, University of California at Los Angeles; Jacques Grospeiller, Paris, France; Ann Harris, Harper & Row, Publishers, New York City; Dr. Hwang Chien-Hou, Professor of Psychology, Taiwan Normal University, Taipei; Alan Jacobs, Chairman, Department of Anthropology, University of Michigan, Kalamazoo; Margaret A. Kelley, Associate Social Affairs Officer, Social Development Division of the United Nations, New York City; Ida Magli, Faculty of Literature and Cultural Anthropology, Rome University, Italy; Marzia Malli, Milan, Italy; Mrs. Fatima Meer, Department of Sociology, University of Natal, South Africa; Jean-François Moreaux, Press Attaché, I.N.S.E.E., Paris, France; Angela Podkaneni, Associate Professor of Psychology, Catholic University, Rio de Janeiro, Brazil; Filippo Ruggieri, Director of Medical Services, Ravasini Organon S.P.A., Rome, Italy; Ingrit Stever, Bonn, Germany; Antonio Tamburello, Director, Skinner Institute, Rome, Italy; United Nations Population Division, New York City; Dr. Yeh En-Kung, Professor of Psychiatry, National Taiwan University, Taipei.

Index

Numerals in italics indicate a photograph or drawing of the subject mentioned.

Depression, 47, 107, 109, 135, 157
Deutscher, Max, 83-85
DeVaron, Tina, 43-46
Developmental period(s), 22, 24
Divorce, 80, *88-99*
Dream, occupational, 69, 71
Driver's license, as milestone, 28, 32, 42

E

Early adulthood era, 22
Ego, 12
Elderly. *See* Old age; Retirement
Elderly, care of: in China, 148; in Europe,
148; by governments, 148, 149; in Japan,
148; in Lawrence, Kansas, 149-150;
medical, 149, 150, 154; in middle years,
109; in nursing homes, *146-147*, 149, 150;
in Oriental households, 148, 154-156; with
personal assistance, 148-154; in Sweden,
150-154; in United States, 148-149
Elkind, David, 17-18
Engagement period, 79-80
Erikson, Erik H., *16*; adolescent stage of, 15,
41, 42, 50, 59-62; childhood stages of, 15;
crisis theory of, 15-19, 121; generativity
concept of, 18, 121; identity concept of,
18-19, 27; life-cycle theory of, 15-19, 27; old
age stage of, 18-19, 157; psychosocial
moratorium of, *58*, 59-*62*; psychosocial
phases of, 15; view of death of, 157; young
adulthood stage of, 18, 67-68
Estrogen, 105-106, 109
Ethical sense, in adolescence, 50,
55-57
Extended family(ies), 103

F

Fang, of West Africa, 85
Fidelity, as virtue, 15
Follicle-stimulating hormone (FSH), 105
Fountain of Youth, *23*
Frank, Anne, 41
Freud, Sigmund: emphasis of, on childhood,
12, 15; genital maturity concept of, 40-41;
Jung's disagreement with, 16, 72; marital
choice theory of, 78; as mentor of Jung, 12,
72; as precursor of life-cycle theorists, 12;
as protegé of Breuer, 72; psychosexual
phases of, 15
Friedenberg, Edgar, 49
Fuller, Jack, *115, 117*

G

Gallup poll, of prestige occupations, 71
Gandhi, Mahatma, 119-121
Generation gap, 42, 48-49, 50, *56*
Generativity, 18, 121
Genital maturity, 40-41
Genital phase, 15
Gerontology, 8

Ginzberg, Eli, 69-70
Goal(s), 9
Gould, Roger, *17*, 27; findings of, 24, *graphs*
41, *graphs* 69, *graphs* 103; studies by, 19,
24
Grabowicz, Anna Ludmilla, *20-21*
Gray Panthers, 136
Great Depression, of 1930s, 134
Greenfield, Josh, 110
Groffman, Karl, 9, 12
Group for the Advancement of Psychiatry, 64,
65
Guthrie, Joseph, *138*

H

Halbstarken, 46
Harden, Theodore A., *139*
Hare Krishna movement, 41
Hart, Ed, 19
Hayflick, Leonard, 140
Health: and adaptation, 148; care, 26, *124-
125*; concern for, *graph* 69; facilities for, in
retirement community, *124-125*; in midlife,
110; in old age, 148-149; in retirement,
135-136
Helford, Sam, *125*
Hero worship, *43*
Hess, Robert, 50
Hindu wedding, 28, *32*; choice of mate, *81*
Holmes, Oliver Wendell, Jr., 27
Home for Aged and Infirm Hebrews, New
York City, 149
Home Samaritans, of Sweden, 150
Homosexuality, temporary, adolescent, 41-42
Hope, as virtue, 15
Hot flash(es), 105-106, 109

I

Idealism, of adolescence, 55, *60-61*
Identity: by adolescents, 41, 42; confusion,
16; Erikson's concept of, 15-17, 41; James's
definition of, 17; negative, 17; redefinition
of, in old age, 143-144
Illness(es), psychosomatic: in midlife crisis,
112; in retirement syndrome, 135
Income, insecurity about, *graph* 69
Independence, as adolescent goal, 41, 42-50;
characteristics of phase of, 42
India: birth-control promotion in, *86*; life
expectancy in, *graph* 155; mate selection in
village of, *81*
Individuation, 13, 16
Indonesia, *graph* 155
Infidelity, 112
Integrated personality type, 145
Integrity, 18-19, 27
Intellectual ability(ies): in old age, 141, 143;
of young adulthood, 68
Intellectualization, adolescent, 41
Intimacy, 67-68

Involutional melancholia, 107
Isolation, 67-68
Ivory Coast, of Africa, celebration of
childbearing in, *28-29*

J

James, William, 17
Japan: care of elderly in, 148; life expectancy
in, 8, *graph* 155; mate selection in, 75;
pensions in, 135, 154; population
distribution in, 8, *graph* 11; reward for
birth of child in, 85; treatment of death in,
156
Johnson, Luci, 59
Johnson, Virginia, 140-141
Josselyn, Irene, 46, 51
Jung, Carl Gustav, *16*; collective unconscious
theory of, 13; disagreement of, with Freud,
16, 72; ego formation stage of, 12-13; as
father of life-cycle theory, 12,16;
individuation process of, 13, 16; life-cycle
theory of, 12-13; marital choice theory of,
78; as protegé of Freud, 12, 72; self-
realization theory of, 13
Jurgen, Hans, 75-78
Jury, Dan and Mark, *158-159, 160, 164, 166-
167, 168-169*

K

Kagan, Jerome, 42, 43-46
Kahn, Robert, 149
Kansas City Study of Adult Life, 144
Keniston, Kenneth, 46, 50-57
Kinsey, Alfred, 112
Kohlberg, Lawrence, 57
Kübler-Ross, Elisabeth, 157
Kuhn, Maggie, *136*

L

Late adulthood era, 22
Late, late adulthood era, 22
Latent phase, 15
Lawrence, Kansas, services for elderly in,
149-150
Leiber, Judith, 83
LeMasters, E. E., 85
Levinson, Daniel J., life-cycle theory of, *17*, 19-
24; age 30 transition, 87; developmental
periods, 22; early adulthood era, 22, 28, 68,
87; eras of life cycle, 22; late adulthood
era, 22; life-structure view, 22, 68; mentor
figure, 71-72; middle adulthood era, 22-24,
102; midlife transition, 114-119; periods of
stability, 22; periods of transition, 22-23,
114-119; pre-adulthood era, 22;
reestablishment process, 114-119; settling-
down period, 87; "special (loved and
loving) woman," 72; studies by, 19;
symbolic rebirth, 119-121
Lewis, Meriwether, 121

United Nations: age profiles of, *graph* 11; life expectancy figures of, *graph* 155

University of Pennsylvania, study of causes of dissension by, 80-81

V

Vaillant, George, 12, 71

Values, search for, in adolescence, 41, 50-57, 60; by activists, 55, *60-61*; cynicism in, 50-55; ethical sense in, 50, 55-57; moral development in, 55-57

Vietnam Summer, 55

Virility, as Roman life-cycle segment, 10

Virtue(s), of life-cycle stages, 15-19

Voting, as milestone, *32*, 42

W

Watt, James, 63

Wedding, Hindu, 28, *32*

Weiss, Robert, 74

West Germany: birth rate of, 11; life expectancy in, 11, *graph* 155; population distribution of, *graph* 11

Weyne, Vladia, 103

Whistler, James McNeill, 70

Will, as virtue, 15

Wirth, Sol, 111-112

Wisdom: components of, 143; in old age, 143; as virtue, 18

Woman, special (loved and loving), 72

Women: conflicts of, 67, 109; cues to onset of midlife of, 102; freedom of, in midlife, 113-114; life expectancy of, *graph* 157; midlife problems of, 109; optimum age of, for motherhood, 68; single, 82. *See also* Climacteric; Menopause

World War II veterans, study of, 15

Y

Yeomans, George, *126*

Young adulthood, 7-8, 67-87; abilities in, 68; of Aymara Indians of Brazil, 69; birth control in, 83, *86*; career choice in, 68-73; career mobility in, 103; children in, 83, 85; choices of, 67, 68, 73, 78-79, 83, *84*, 87, 88; concerns of, 7-8, *graphs* 69; conflict in, 18, 67-68; crisis in, 85, 87; the dream of, 69; Erikson's view of, 18, 67-68; forming an occupation in, 69-73; Gould's description of, 24; Levinson's view of, 68, 69, 71-73; life structure as goal of, 68; marital relations in, *graph* 69, 80-82; marriage decision in, 73-74; mate selection in, 74-80, *76-77*; "the mentor" in, 71; of Myakusa of Africa, 69; occupational choice in, 68-73; physical prowess in, *72-73*; pregnancy in, 83-85, *92-93*; in simple societies, 26; single people in, 74, 82; transition periods in, 23; in Western cultures, 7-8

Youth, as Roman life-cycle segment, 10

Youth culture, 63

Yurok Indians, of America, 15-16